Happy Birthday

from

Grandma

Southern Living

The SOUTHERN HERITAGE COOKBOOK LIBRARY

The SOUTHERN HERITAGE
Company's Coming!
COOKBOOK

OXMOOR HOUSE
Birmingham, Alabama

Southern Living.

The Southern Heritage Cookbook Library

Copyright 1983 by Oxmoor House, Inc.
Book Division of Southern Progress Corporation
P.O. Box 2262, Birmingham, Alabama 35201

Southern Living® is a federally registered trademark belonging to
Southern Living, Inc.

Library of Congress Catalog Number: 82-062140
ISBN:0-8487-0603-X

Manufactured in the United States of America

The Southern Heritage COMPANY'S COMING! Cookbook

Manager, Editorial Projects: Ann H. Harvey
Southern Living® *Foods Editor*: Jean W. Liles
Production Editor: Joan E. Denman
Foods Editor: Katherine M. Eakin
Director, Test Kitchen: Laura N. Nestelroad
Test Kitchen Home Economists: Pattie B. Booker,
   Elizabeth J. Taliaferro, Kay E. Clarke, Nancy Nevins
Production Manager: Jerry R. Higdon
Copy Editor: Melinda E. West
Editorial Assistant: Karen P. Traccarella
Food Photographer: Jim Bathie
Food Stylist: Sara Jane Ball
Layout Designer: Christian von Rosenvinge
Mechanical Artist: Faith Nance
Research Assistant: Janice Randall

Special Consultants

Art Director: Irwin Glusker
Heritage Consultant: Meryle Evans
Foods Writer: Lillian B. Marshall
Food and Recipe Consultants: Marilyn Wyrick Ingram,
   Audrey P. Stehle

Cover Menu begins on page 94. Photograph by George Ratkai.

CONTENTS

INTRODUCTION

t is easy to see why the Southerner has always loved company. Farms and ranches were far apart, towns were few and far between, and transportation was arduous. To have company was to revel in the transient guest and his stories of other places he'd been and perhaps news of mutual acquaintances. From Day One in the South, "company's coming" has been the signal to "put the big pot in the little one." Here are menus that recapture the hospitality of the Virginia plantation and the Big Sky country of Texas. Creole eye-openers, extravagant teas, and that Depression phenomenon, the tearoom, are here to be enjoyed all over again.

By the late 1600s and early 1700s, the Eastern colonies had oases of elegance and civilization. The French founded New Orleans in 1764, but that part of the country was a separate entity; the two cultures knew little of one another. Yet the French, then Spanish, then Creole tradition was also one of open-handed hospitality.

From that first Virginia landfall, the movement through the South and westward into Texas and Oklahoma took over two hundred years. Men who were to become the cattle barons of Texas and the oil tycoons of Oklahoma left comfort behind and went looking for new lands, pushing the frontier ahead of them. German immigrants, arriving in Texas in the mid-1800s, came into the same hardscrabble way of life. Then, out of hardship, a flowering.

At their Matador Ranch in Motley County, Texas, the H.H. Campbells started a Christmas dinner tradition in the late 1800s that lasted three-quarters of a century. Neighboring ranchers (the nearest was over twenty miles away) and all their cowboys were invited to a feast that took Lizzie Campbell a week to produce.

General Robert E. Lee visited the King Ranch several times between 1856 and 1861 and was entertained most royally. Lee was in the enviable position of understanding Southern hospitality all the way from the well-entrenched traditions of coastal society to the rough and ready Southwest brand that, based on different circumstances, made up its rules as it went along. But wherever you live, company's on the way! Let's give them a real Southern welcome.

YE OLDE TRADITIONS

From the Eastern Seaboard to the Texas Hills

Dining Room in the Judge Robert Pringle House, Charleston, South Carolina.

The varied culinary backgrounds Southerners have to draw upon is remarkably regional, even today. For example, "Plantation cooking" has to be qualified: Are we discussing the Virginia-English cuisine along the James River or the French-based, African-improved foods of the Cane River country of northern Louisiana?

The Amerindian influence was not the same in every part of the South. The cooking done by various tribes differed because of geography, climate, and terrain. Settled tribes farmed corn and other vegetables. Hunting peoples developed trails and carried pemmican, a mixture not unlike modern backpackers' dried food. Smoke curing, frying on hot stones, roasting before open fires, and ash cookery were in general use but in the Southwest, the Pueblos had adobe ovens. Then came the Spanish-Mexican influence with chiles and herbs, and presto! Barbecue! The Texas hill country is famous for it.

The Moravians of North Carolina and the Shakers of Kentucky were religious groups who left profound marks on Southern cooking. The Germanic Moravians settled what the coastal aristocracy called the "back country" in the mid-1700s. Their cooking is reminiscent of the Pennsylvania Dutch, a stamp that lingers after two hundred years.

In Low Country Charleston and Savannah, shrimp has been a traditional part of breakfast. But don't ask for sweetened rice; the consequences could be dreadful. In Kentucky or Texas, rice may be sugared without raising eyebrows.

Along the cypress-shaded banks of the James River are to be found some of this country's most monumentally beautiful plantation houses. Carter's Grove, built by Carter Burwell in the mid 1750s, can be seen via an easy side trip out of Williamsburg. Shirley Plantation dates back to the early eighteenth century. Once the home of Robert E. Lee's grandfather, Charles Carter, it has housed ten generations of the Carter family. Owners of these and other plantations kept in touch by water in the early days, navigating among the cypress knees that edge the river, and entertaining lavishly.

Menus in this chapter illustrate the many ways we cook Southern: Creole, coastal, ranch-style . . . and our food is always flavored by our own grandmothers' wisdom.

DINNER ON THE JAMES RIVER

The English have always loved mutton and, after a few false starts, established sheep in the new land. Along the James River, descendants of colonists still serve lamb as well as that ancient balm to the British palate, plum pudding.

Southerners take their delicious Sally Lunn bread and its variations for granted, perhaps forgetting there really was a Sally Lunn. In the seventeenth century, she was a baker in Bath and "cried" her wares in the streets of the fashionable spa. Her home still stands in the town and houses a tearoom and a charming gift shop.

COLD VEGETABLE SOUP
ROASTED LEG OF LAMB WITH
OVEN-BROWNED POTATOES
BUTTERED BEETS
BRAISED BROCCOLI IN TOMATO CUPS
SALLY LUNN MUFFINS
PINEAPPLE POUND CAKE
PLUM PUDDING WITH SHERRIED HARD SAUCE
BOURBON CAKE

Serves 8

COLD VEGETABLE SOUP

3 cups chicken broth
1½ cups diced white potatoes
1½ cups English peas
¼ cup plus 2 tablespoons minced green onion
¼ teaspoon celery salt
¼ teaspoon curry powder
¾ cup whipping cream

Combine first 4 ingredients in a Dutch oven. Cover and simmer about 20 minutes or until vegetables are tender. Cool. Stir in celery salt and curry powder.

Place in container of electric blender, and process until smooth. Stir in whipping cream. Chill at least 3 hours. Yield: 8 servings.

ROASTED LEG OF LAMB WITH OVEN-BROWNED POTATOES

1 (7- to 9-pound) leg of lamb
4 cloves garlic, sliced
¾ teaspoon pepper, divided
8 medium potatoes, peeled and halved
¼ teaspoon dried whole rosemary
¼ cup chopped fresh parsley
½ cup thinly sliced celery
2 tablespoons butter or margarine
2 tablespoons lemon juice
½ teaspoon salt

Remove the fell (tissue-like covering) from lamb with a sharp knife. Make several small slits on outside of lamb, and stuff with garlic slices. Sprinkle with ½ teaspoon pepper. Place lamb, fat side up, on a rack in a large roasting pan.

Bake at 325° for 2½ hours. Add potatoes, remaining pepper, and rosemary; bake 1½ hours or until meat thermometer registers 175°. Remove lamb and potatoes to a warm platter; reserve pan drippings.

Sauté parsley and celery in butter in a small saucepan until celery is tender. Add remaining ingredients; cover and simmer 5 minutes. Skim fat from reserved pan drippings. Combine parsley mixture and pan drippings; cook over low heat until heated. Serve with lamb and potatoes. Yield: 8 to 10 servings.

BUTTERED BEETS

4 cups pared, diced fresh beets
3 tablespoons cornstarch
½ cup sugar
¼ cup vinegar
¼ cup butter or margarine

Place beets in a large saucepan; add water to cover. Bring to a boil; cover and cook 15 minutes or until tender. Drain, reserving ½ cup liquid.

Combine next 2 ingredients in a saucepan; slowly stir in reserved liquid. Cook over medium heat, stirring until thickened and bubbly. Remove from heat; stir in vinegar and butter. Pour over beets. Yield: 8 servings.

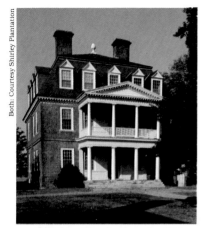

Shirley Plantation, built in the 1730s, and its adjacent buildings along the James River in Virginia.

BRAISED BROCCOLI IN TOMATO CUPS

4 pounds fresh broccoli
  (2 bunches)
5 large firm tomatoes
1 clove garlic, minced
2 tablespoons olive oil
¼ teaspoon salt
⅛ teaspoon pepper
½ cup shredded sharp
  Cheddar cheese

Trim off large leaves of broccoli. Remove stalks; break into flowerets, and wash thoroughly. Cook broccoli, uncovered, in boiling salted water for 8 minutes or until crisp-tender. Drain and place in cold water about 5 minutes; remove and drain well.

Cut tomatoes in half; scoop out pulp, leaving shells intact. Reserve pulp for use in other recipes. Invert tomato shells on paper towels, and set aside.

Sauté garlic in olive oil until lightly browned; remove from heat, and stir in broccoli, salt, and pepper. Arrange broccoli in tomato cups. Sprinkle each with cheese.

Place tomato cups in two 9-inch square baking pans. Bake at 300° for 5 minutes or until cheese melts. Yield: 10 servings.

Note: ½ cup grated Parmesan cheese may be substituted for Cheddar cheese.

SALLY LUNN MUFFINS

1 cup milk, scalded
½ cup butter
⅓ cup sugar
1 teaspoon salt
3 eggs
1 package dry yeast
½ cup warm water (105°
  to 115°)
4 cups all-purpose flour
2 tablespoons butter, melted

Combine milk, ½ cup butter, sugar, and salt in a large mixing bowl; stir until butter melts. Let cool to 105° to 115°. Add eggs, beating well.

Dissolve yeast in warm water, and stir into milk mixture. Add flour, beating until smooth. Cover and let rise in a warm place (85°), free from drafts, 3½ hours or until doubled in bulk.

Beat batter with a wooden spoon until blisters form. Spoon batter into greased muffin pans, filling about one-third full. Cover; let rise in a warm place (85°), free from drafts, 20 minutes or until doubled in bulk.

Brush top of each muffin with melted butter. Bake at 400° for 20 to 25 minutes or until lightly browned. Serve warm. Yield: 2 dozen.

PINEAPPLE POUND CAKE

1 cup vegetable oil
3 cups sugar
6 eggs
3 cups all-purpose flour
1 teaspoon baking powder
Pinch of salt
¾ cup crushed pineapple, undrained
1 teaspoon vanilla extract
Pineapple Glaze

Combine oil and sugar, mixing well. Add eggs, one at a time, beating well after each addition.

Combine flour, baking powder, and salt; gradually add to oil mixture, beating well. Stir in pineapple and vanilla.

Pour batter into a well-greased and floured 10-inch tube pan. Bake at 350° for 1 hour and 25 minutes or until done. Invert pan and cool 10 to 15 minutes; remove from pan, and cool completely. Pour Pineapple Glaze over cake. Yield: one 10-inch cake.

Pineapple Glaze:

2 tablespoons sugar
1½ teaspoons cornstarch
½ cup pineapple juice

Combine sugar and cornstarch in a heavy saucepan; stir well. Add juice, stirring well. Cook over medium heat until thickened and translucent. Cool. Yield: about ½ cup.

19th–century advertisement

PLUM PUDDING WITH SHERRIED HARD SAUCE

3 cups all-purpose flour
1 teaspoon baking soda
½ teaspoon salt
2 teaspoons ground cinnamon
½ teaspoon ground allspice
½ teaspoon ground cloves
2 cups raisins
1 cup peeled, chopped cooking apples
1 cup currants
1 cup light molasses
1 cup cold water
2 cups finely chopped suet
Sherried Hard Sauce

Combine flour, soda, salt, and spices in a large mixing bowl; mix well. Stir in raisins, apple, and currants.

Combine molasses, water, and suet; add to dry ingredients, mixing well. Spoon mixture into a well-greased 2½-quart mold; cover tightly.

Place mold on rack in a large, deep kettle with enough boiling water to come halfway up mold. Cover kettle; steam pudding 3 hours in boiling water, replacing water as needed. Unmold and serve with Sherried Hard Sauce. Refrigerate leftover pudding. Yield: 12 to 14 servings.

Sherried Hard Sauce:

½ cup butter, softened
1 cup sifted powdered sugar
2 tablespoons sherry

Combine butter and sugar; beat until smooth. Add sherry; beat until fluffy. Chill. Yield: ¾ cup.

Note: Pipe hard sauce around base of pudding.

Courtesy Shirley Plantation

The rise of the pineapple as a symbol of hospitality in Colonial times probably came about because of its very rarity. Virginia imported pineapples from the West Indies, but they were available only in August. To procure and to share the exotic treat was indeed an occasion; pineapple was not just something one happened to have lying around the house. It seems appropriate that Shirley Plantation, a bastion of Southern hospitality, has the pineapple finial atop its roof. The motif appears as an architectural element throughout the home.

In addition to the pineapple, Virginia imported oranges, limes, and lemons from Bermuda and the West Indies in the wintertime. It was possible, then, to have fruited wine punches, cakes, and pies for Christmas. Wine was imported at a goodly pace as well, the hands-down favorite being Madeira.

BOURBON CAKE

1 (15-ounce) package raisins, chopped
1 cup candied pineapple, finely chopped
1 (8-ounce) package candied cherries, finely chopped
8 cups chopped pecans
4 cups all-purpose flour, divided
1½ cups butter or margarine, softened
2 cups sugar
6 eggs
2½ teaspoons baking powder
2 teaspoons ground nutmeg
1 cup bourbon
1 cup orange marmalade
½ cup molasses
Candied cherries (optional)

Combine first 4 ingredients; dredge with 1 cup flour, stirring to coat well. Set aside.

Cream butter in a large mixing bowl; gradually add sugar, beating until light and fluffy. Add eggs, one at a time, beating well after each addition.

Combine remaining 3 cups flour, baking powder, and nutmeg; add to creamed mixture alternately with bourbon, marmalade, and molasses; mix well after each addition. Stir in reserved fruit and nuts.

Heavily grease one 10-inch tube pan; line sides and bottom of pan with greased, heavy brown paper. Spoon batter into pan, and bake at 275° for 3½ to 4 hours or until done.

Cool cake completely in pan. Garnish with cherries, if desired. To store, wrap cake in cloth soaked in brandy or bourbon; wrap with plastic or waxed paper; place in a tightly covered tin. Yield: one 10-inch cake.

Handsome dessert buffet at Shirley Plantation: Bourbon Cake (left), Plum Pudding with Sherried Hard Sauce (top), and sliced Pineapple Pound Cake.

Henry Ford Museum. The Edison Institute

SHAKER DAILY FARE

"Give your hands to work and your heart to God." Mother Ann Lee's command motivated the Shakers; labor was sacred. They invented the flat-sided broom, clothespins, the circular saw, and countless other practical objects used in the house and field, many still in use today. Officially neutral during the Civil War, the Shakers at Pleasant Hill, Kentucky, were also geographically in the middle. They felt obliged to feed and shelter troops of both armies, utterly depleting all their supplies. By 1900, Shakers in all eighteen villages in the country numbered only a thousand.

RELISH BOWL * SPICED TOMATO JUICE
COUNTRY STEAK
SPINACH WITH BASIL
GERMAN POTATO SALAD
FRIED GREEN TOMATOES
STRAWBERRY PRESERVES * CARROT PICKLES
WHOLE WHEAT ROLLS
SHAKER WHEATEN BREAD
LEMON PIE

Serves 6

RELISH BOWL

6 stalks celery hearts, cut in half
½ cup small ripe pitted olives
½ cup pimiento-stuffed olives
1 (14-ounce) jar crisp okra pickles
2 (3½-ounce) jars miniature pickled corn
⅓ cup sweet pickle slices
⅓ cup dill pickle slices
1 small head cauliflower, broken into flowerets
2 large cucumbers, unpeeled and sliced
1 (6-ounce) package radishes

Arrange all vegetables in a large bowl. Yield: 6 servings.

An appetizing relish tray at Shakertown: Crisp fresh vegetables, olives, and pickled okra.

SPICED TOMATO JUICE

1 (48-ounce) can tomato juice
2 teaspoons Worcestershire sauce
1¾ teaspoon salt
1 teaspoon seasoned salt
1 teaspoon hot sauce
½ cup whipping cream, whipped

Combine tomato juice, Worcestershire sauce, and seasonings in a large saucepan. Bring to a boil; reduce heat, and simmer 5 minutes. Cover and chill completely.

Serve with a dollop of whipped cream. Yield: 6 servings.

A nineteenth-century Shaker kitchen: model of efficiency.

COUNTRY STEAK

3 pounds boneless round
  steak, 1½- to 1¾-inches
  thick
½ cup all-purpose flour
2 tablespoons
  shortening
1 teaspoon salt
¼ teaspoon pepper
1 tablespoon Worcestershire
  sauce
1 cup chopped celery
½ cup chopped onions
2 cups beef broth
½ cup catsup
6 whole cloves

Trim excess fat from steak;
sprinkle flour evenly on both
sides of steak, and pound with a
meat mallet.

Melt shortening in a large
Dutch oven; brown steak on
both sides. Combine remaining
ingredients, stirring well; pour
over steak. Cover and bake at
350° for 2 to 2½ hours or until
tender, adding more water, if
necessary. Yield: 6 servings.

SPINACH WITH BASIL

4 pounds fresh spinach
6 sprigs parsley, chopped
4 green onions, chopped
¼ cup butter or margarine
2 teaspoons salt
½ teaspoon pepper
1 teaspoon dried whole
  basil

Remove stems from spinach;
wash leaves thoroughly, and
tear into pieces. Place all ingredients in a large Dutch oven (do
not add water). Cover, and cook
over medium-high heat for 5
minutes or until spinach is
limp. Yield: 6 servings.

GERMAN POTATO SALAD

7 medium-size new
  potatoes
3 slices bacon
1 small onion, chopped
½ cup water
½ cup vinegar
1 tablespoon sugar
2 teaspoons cornstarch
1 teaspoon salt

Scrub potatoes. Cook in boiling water 30 minutes or until
tender. Drain, and chill well.
Peel and cut potatoes into thin
slices.

Cook bacon in a large skillet
until done but still limp. Remove bacon, reserving drippings in skillet. Tear bacon into
bite-size pieces; set aside.

Sauté onion in bacon drippings until tender. Stir in remaining ingredients; cook over
medium heat until slightly
thickened. Add bacon and pour
over potatoes. Toss gently.
Yield: 6 servings.

15

Good

FRIED GREEN TOMATOES

½ cup cornmeal
¼ teaspoon sugar
½ teaspoon salt
⅛ teaspoon pepper
6 medium-size green
   tomatoes, cut into ¼-inch
   slices
About ½ cup vegetable oil

Combine cornmeal, sugar, salt, and pepper; stir well. Dredge tomatoes in cornmeal mixture.

Heat oil in a large skillet to 375°; add tomatoes and fry until golden brown on each side. Drain on paper towels. Yield: 6 to 8 servings.

Nineteenth-century seed boxes from Shakertown.

STRAWBERRY PRESERVES

1½ quarts strawberries
5 cups sugar
⅓ cup lemon juice

Wash and hull strawberries. Combine strawberries and sugar in a large Dutch oven; stir gently to avoid bruising berries; let stand 3 to 4 hours.

Slowly bring strawberry mixture to a boil, stirring occasionally until sugar dissolves. Stir in lemon juice. Boil 12 minutes or until berries are clear, stirring occasionally. Remove from heat, and skim off foam with a metal spoon.

Carefully remove fruit from syrup with a slotted spoon, and place in a shallow pan. Bring syrup to a boil; cook about 10 minutes or until syrup has thickened to desired consistency. Pour syrup over fruit. Let stand, uncovered, 12 to 24 hours in a cool place. Shake pan occasionally (do not stir) to allow berries to absorb syrup and remain plump and whole. Skim off foam.

Ladle preserves into hot sterilized jars, leaving ¼-inch headspace; cover at once with metal lids, and screw bands tight. Process in boiling-water bath 20 minutes. Yield: 4 half pints.

CARROT PICKLES

4 cups sliced carrots
2 medium onions, sliced
¾ cup sugar
¾ teaspoon salt
½ teaspoon ground cinnamon
¼ teaspoon ground ginger
¼ teaspoon ground cloves
¼ teaspoon celery seeds
1 tablespoon vegetable oil
2 cups vinegar

Place carrots and onions in a saucepan, and add water to cover. Bring to a boil; reduce heat and simmer 5 minutes. Drain.

Add remaining ingredients, and bring to a boil. Reduce heat, and simmer 10 minutes.

Pack into hot sterilized jars, leaving ¼-inch headspace. Cover at once with metal lids, and screw bands tight. Process in boiling-water bath for 10 minutes. Yield: 2 pints.

WHOLE WHEAT ROLLS

2 packages dry yeast
2 cups warm milk (105°
   to 115°)
1 egg
½ cup sugar
1½ teaspoons salt
3½ cups whole wheat flour
1 cup plus 1 tablespoon
   shortening, melted
3½ cups all-purpose flour
3 tablespoons melted butter
   or margarine

Dissolve yeast in milk in a large bowl. Stir in egg, sugar, and salt. Add whole wheat flour and shortening, mixing well. Gradually add all-purpose flour to form a stiff dough, beating well after each addition.

Place dough in a lightly greased bowl, turning to grease top. Cover and let rise in a warm place (85°), free from drafts, for 1½ hours or until doubled in bulk. Punch down; cover and let rise 30 minutes or until doubled in bulk.

Lightly grease muffin pans. Shape dough into 2-inch balls; place 1 ball in each muffin cup. Brush tops with melted butter. Cover, and let rise 45 minutes or until doubled in bulk. Bake at 400° for 12 to 15 minutes or until golden brown. Yield: about 3 dozen.

SHAKER WHEATEN BREAD

2 packages dry yeast
1 cup warm water (105°
  to 115°), divided
1 cup milk, scalded
3 tablespoons butter or
  margarine
¼ cup honey
1 tablespoon salt
2 cups all-purpose flour
4 cups whole wheat flour
2 tablespoons butter or
  margarine, melted

Dissolve yeast in ¼ cup water; let stand 5 minutes. Combine milk, butter, honey, salt, and remaining water in a bowl; mix well. Cool. Add yeast mixture; mix well. Gradually stir in flour.

Turn dough out onto a floured surface, and knead 8 to 10 minutes or until smooth and elastic. Place in a well-greased bowl, turning to grease top. Cover and let rise in a warm place (85°), free from drafts, 50 to 60 minutes or until doubled in bulk.

Punch dough down, and place in two well-greased 8½- x 4½- x 3-inch loafpans. Brush top with melted butter. Cover and let rise in a warm, draft-free place (85°) 1 hour or until doubled in bulk. Bake at 350° for 55 to 60 minutes or until loaf sounds hollow when tapped. Yield: 2 loaves.

Shaker lady slicing bread.

Leslie's Illustrated. September 13, 1873

*Shaker favorites served with Strawberry Preserves:
Whole Wheat Rolls and Shaker Wheaten Bread.*

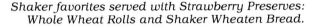

LEMON PIE

Double-crust pastry (recipe
  follows)
1 tablespoon lemon rind
2 lemons, peeled, seeded, and
  thinly sliced
2 cups sugar
4 eggs, slightly beaten

Roll half of pastry to ⅛-inch thickness, and fit into a 9-inch pieplate.

Combine lemon rind, slices, and sugar, stirring well. Let stand at least 1 hour. Add eggs, stirring well.

Pour into pastry-lined pieplate. Cover with top crust, and slit in several places to allow steam to escape; seal and flute edges. Bake at 450° for 15 minutes; reduce temperature to 375°, and continue baking for 20 minutes. Cool before serving. Yield: one 9-inch pie.

Double-crust pastry:

2 cups all-purpose flour
½ teaspoon salt
⅔ cup shortening
5 to 6 tablespoons cold water

Combine flour and salt; cut in shortening with pastry blender until mixture resembles coarse meal. Sprinkle cold water evenly over surface; stir with a fork until all dry ingredients are moistened. Shape dough into a ball; chill. Yield: pastry for one double-crust 9-inch pie.

MORAVIAN DINNER

The traditions of thrift and good cooking the Moravians brought to Old Salem is an integral part of Winston-Salem today. The Moravians of Wachovia, now Forsyth County, were the salt traders of "back country" North Carolina. With wagon loads of beeswax, hides, and butter, they made hazardous trips to the East Coast to barter for salt. Neighbors up to a hundred miles away depended on them for the precious commodity. Moravian cooking has a German accent; note the tart recipe and its name—citron is the German word for lemon.

CHICKEN AND COUNTRY HAM DEEP DISH PIE
SAVORY POLE BEANS
MORAVIAN SPICED APPLES
CABBAGE SALAD
CITRON TARTS * MORAVIAN TEA CAKES

Serves 6 to 8

CHICKEN AND COUNTRY HAM DEEP DISH PIE

2 (2½- to 3-pound)
   broiler-fryers
1 tablespoon salt
1 teaspoon pepper
1 teaspoon ground thyme
1 teaspoon rubbed sage
Pastry (recipe follows)
¼ cup butter or margarine,
   divided
2 tablespoons all-purpose
   flour
1 slice country ham, cut into
   1-inch pieces

Place chicken, salt, pepper, thyme, and sage in a large Dutch oven; add water to cover. Bring to a boil; cover and simmer 1 hour or until tender. Remove chicken, reserving 1 cup broth; cool chicken. Remove chicken from bone, and cut into bite-size pieces.

Line a 2-quart baking dish with two-thirds of pastry. Place chicken in pastry shell.

Melt 2 tablespoons butter in a medium saucepan; add flour, stirring until smooth. Cook 1 minute, stirring constantly. Gradually stir in broth; cook over medium heat, stirring constantly, until thickened and bubbly. Pour sauce evenly over chicken.

Place ham pieces over chicken mixture, and dot with remaining butter. Top with remaining pastry. Trim edges of pastry; seal and crimp edges. Cut slits to allow steam to escape. Decorate with pastry cutouts, if desired. Bake at 400° for 40 minutes or until crust is golden brown. Yield: about 8 servings.

Pastry:

3 cups all-purpose flour
1 teaspoon salt
1 cup shortening
5 to 6 tablespoons ice water

Combine flour and salt in a bowl; cut in shortening with pastry blender until mixture resembles coarse meal. Sprinkle cold water evenly over surface; stir with a fork until all dry ingredients are moistened. Roll dough to ⅛-inch thickness on a lightly floured surface. Yield: pastry for one 2-quart casserole.

SAVORY POLE BEANS

2 pounds fresh pole beans
1 small clove garlic
¼ cup cooking oil
1 cup chopped green
   pepper
6 slices onion
2 teaspoons salt
1 to 1½ teaspoons dried
   whole basil
1 teaspoon sugar
½ cup boiling water
¼ cup grated Parmesan
   cheese

Remove strings from beans; cut beans into 1-inch pieces, and wash.

Sauté garlic in hot oil until tender; remove and discard. Add green pepper and onion to hot oil, and sauté about 3 minutes over low heat or until tender. Add salt, basil, sugar, and water. Cover, and cook over low heat for 15 minutes or until beans are tender. Sprinkle with cheese. Yield: 8 servings.

Create a beautiful meal around Chicken and Country Ham Deep Dish Pie, ending with famous Moravian sweets.

MORAVIAN SPICED APPLES

8 medium-size baking apples
2 cups water
¼ cup sugar
1 (2-inch) stick cinnamon
2 whole cloves
6 drops red food coloring

Core and peel apples, reserving peel. Combine apple peel and water in a large saucepan. Bring water to a boil; reduce heat to low, and cook until apple peel is tender. Remove peel.

Add remaining ingredients to water, and bring to a boil; reduce heat to low, and add apples. Cook for 35 minutes or until apples are tender, basting occasionally with syrup.

Remove from heat, and let cool completely. Cover, and refrigerate over night. Yield: 6 to 8 servings.

CABBAGE SALAD

3 eggs
¼ cup plus 2 tablespoons vinegar
⅛ teaspoon dry mustard
¼ cup butter or margarine, softened
1 medium cabbage, shredded

Combine eggs, vinegar, and mustard in top of double boiler; beat until frothy. Place over boiling water; cook until mixture thickens. Stir in butter; cool. Pour over cabbage and toss; chill thoroughly. Yield: 6 to 8 servings.

CITRON TARTS

6 egg yolks
¼ cup butter or margarine
1 cup firmly packed light brown sugar
1 tablespoon lemon rind
2 teaspoons lemon juice
Pastry for a 9-inch pie

Place yolks in bowl; cut in butter with a pastry blender. Cut in sugar, lemon rind, and juice. Do not stir. Set aside.

Roll dough to ⅛-inch thickness on a lightly floured surface. Line 4 fluted tart pans with pastry. Fill each with lemon mixture. Bake at 375° for 25 minutes or until set; cool. Yield: four (4-inch) tarts.

Note: Do not double recipe; repeat to serve larger crowds.

MORAVIAN TEA CAKES

1 cup butter or margarine, softened
2 cups sugar
3 eggs
2 tablespoons buttermilk
1 teaspoon baking soda
1 teaspoon salt
1 teaspoon vanilla
5½ cups all-purpose flour

Cream butter; gradually add sugar, beating well. Add eggs, one at a time, beating well after each addition.

Combine next 4 ingredients; stir well. Add to creamed mixture alternately with flour, beginning and ending with flour. Chill dough for 2 hours.

Roll dough out onto a lightly floured surface to ½-inch thickness; cut out with 2½-inch heart-shaped cookie cutter. Place on lightly greased cookie sheets. Bake at 375° for 8 minutes or until lightly browned. Yield: about 6 dozen.

DINING IN THE LOW COUNTRY

South Carolina has been called the Palmetto State, the Rice State, and the Iodine State. Pick any name, but the eastern part belongs, culinarily, to the Low Country where shrimp is king. Or is rice the king? In any event, combine the two for a pilau, and call it perloo.

The three o'clock dinner is not unknown in Charleston, even today. Dinner is soup, meat or fish, rice in some form, two vegetables, and dessert. Since the humid or "giffy" weather makes pastry unpredictable, a baked meringue forms the base for the luscious lemon cream in this menu.

COLD CUCUMBER SOUP
PLANTATION SHRIMP PILAU
CARROT RING MOLD
GREEN PEAS
CRISP CORN STICKS
LEMON CREAM MERINGUE

Serves 6 to 8

Good.

COLD CUCUMBER SOUP

3 tablespoons butter or margarine
2 medium onions, chopped
2 (13½-ounce) cans chicken broth, undiluted
2 medium potatoes, peeled and cubed
1½ tablespoons chopped fresh parsley
2 teaspoons dry mustard
½ teaspoon salt
¼ teaspoon pepper
3 large cucumbers, unpeeled and sliced
1 cup half-and-half
Cucumber slices

Melt butter in a large saucepan. Add onion; sauté 10 minutes or until tender. Add broth, potatoes, parsley, mustard, salt, and pepper; cook over low heat 30 minutes or until potatoes are tender.

Combine potato mixture and cucumber in container of an electric blender; process 3 to 4 minutes or until pureed. Chill at least 4 hours.

Stir in half-and-half before serving; garnish with cucumber slices. Yield: 8 cups.

Cold Cucumber Soup starts a Low Country dinner. Add Crisp Corn Sticks, Carrot Ring Mold containing green peas, and delicious Plantation Shrimp Pilau.

PLANTATION SHRIMP PILAU

6 slices bacon
2 cups water
1 teaspoon salt
1 cup regular rice, uncooked
3 cups shrimp, peeled and deveined
2 teaspoons Worcestershire sauce
1 tablespoon all-purpose flour
¾ cup chopped celery
¼ cup chopped green pepper
3 tablespoons butter or margarine
1 teaspoon salt
½ teaspoon pepper

Fry bacon in large skillet until crisp. Drain bacon, reserving 3 tablespoons drippings. Crumble bacon, and set aside.

Combine water, salt, and drippings in a large saucepan. Bring to a boil; stir in rice. Reduce heat; cover and cook 20 minutes.

Sprinkle shrimp with Worcestershire sauce; dredge in flour. Sauté shrimp, celery, and green pepper in butter for 3 minutes. Cover and cook 2 minutes. Remove from heat, and stir into rice. Add salt, pepper, and reserved bacon, stirring well. Serve hot. Yield: 6 to 8 servings.

CARROT RING MOLD

3 cups mashed cooked
   carrots (about 1½ pounds)
1½ cups cracker crumbs
1½ cups half-and-half
1 cup (4 ounces) shredded
   extra-sharp Cheddar cheese
⅓ cup butter or margarine,
   melted
1 small onion, grated
1½ teaspoons sugar
1½ teaspoons salt
½ teaspoon pepper
4 eggs

Combine first 9 ingredients in a large mixing bowl; mix well, and set aside.

Beat eggs 1 minute at high speed of an electric mixer until frothy and thickened. Gently fold eggs into carrot mixture.

Spoon mixture into a well-greased 1½-quart ring mold. Bake at 350° for 45 minutes. Remove from oven; cool on wire rack 20 minutes.

Invert carrot ring onto serving platter. Yield: 8 servings.

Note: The fresh green peas may be served in center of carrot ring, if desired.

GREEN PEAS

1 cup water
4 cups shelled fresh
   green peas
1 head lettuce, shredded
1 parsley sprig
4 green onions, sliced
¼ cup butter or margraine
1 tablespoon heavy cream
1 teaspoon sugar
¾ teaspoon salt

Bring water to a boil in a large saucepan; add peas, lettuce, parsley, onions, and butter. Bring to a boil; cover, reduce heat, and cook 30 minutes or until tender. Remove parsley. Stir in heavy cream, sugar, and salt; cook 1 minute. Yield: 6 to 8 servings.

Lithograph of Charleston, 1850, with its homes built along the Battery overlooking the harbor and Fort Sumter.

CRISP CORN STICKS

1 cup yellow cornmeal
¼ teaspoon salt
¼ teaspoon baking soda
¼ cup vegetable oil
2 tablespoons light corn
   syrup
1 cup buttermilk

Combine first 3 ingredients in a mixing bowl; set aside.

Combine oil, corn syrup, and buttermilk; mix well. Stir into dry ingredients.

Place a well-greased cast-iron corn stick pan in 400° oven for 3 minutes or until a drop of water sizzles when dropped on pan. Remove pan from oven; spoon batter into pan, filling each section one-half full. Bake at 400° for 25 to 30 minutes or until golden brown. Yield: 1 dozen.

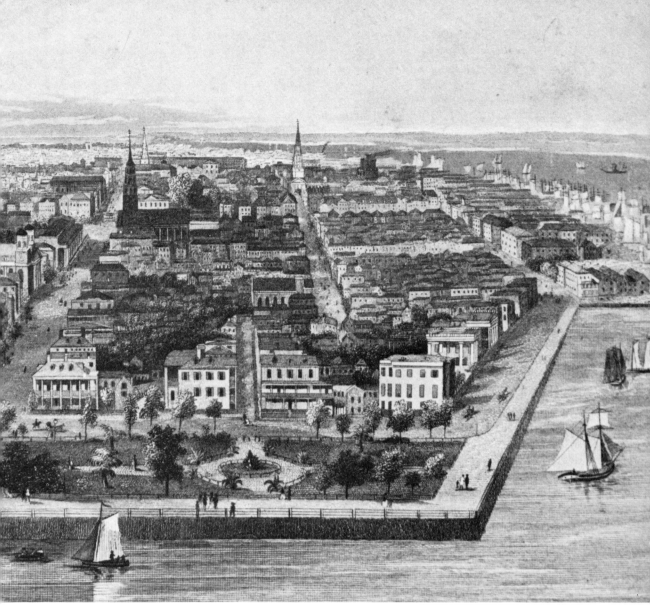

LEMON CREAM MERINGUE

4 eggs, separated
½ teaspoon cream of tartar
1½ cups sugar, divided
2 teaspoons grated lemon
　rind
3 tablespoons lemon juice
2 cups whipping cream,
　divided
1 tablespoon sugar

Combine egg whites (at room temperature) and cream of tartar; beat at medium speed of an electric mixer until foamy. Gradually add 1 cup sugar, 1 tablespoon at a time, beating until stiff peaks form. Spread meringue in a lightly greased 9-inch pieplate. Bake at 300° for 40 minutes or until lightly browned; let cool completely away from drafts.

Beat egg yolks in top of double boiler until thick and lemon colored. Add remaining ½ cup sugar, lemon rind, and juice. Cook over boiling water, stirring constantly, for 5 minutes or until thick. Remove from heat, and let mixture cool completely.

Beat 1 cup whipping cream until soft peaks form; fold into lemon mixture. Spoon into meringue pie shell; refrigerate overnight.

To serve, beat remaining 1 cup whipping cream until foamy. Gradually add 1 tablespoon sugar, and continue beating until soft peaks form. Spread whipped cream over filling. Yield: 6 to 8 servings.

23

FROM THE CANE RIVER

Proof that regional cooking lives is the cuisine of the Cane River country of northern Louisiana. Creole food blends French and Spanish with African; Cajuns, isolated from outside, remained French, save for some Indian influence. But cooking on the "Joyous Coast" of the Cane is a blend of the French and African influences producing such innovations as antelope steak with French sauce and coon gumbo. The Melrose Plantation Big House, built in 1833 by Louis Metoyer, Jr., was a mecca for artists and writers who feasted on foods such as this menu suggests.

BASS À LA BRIN
POTATO MARRAINE (Potato Puffs)
or
RIZ ISLE BREVELLE (Rice Croquettes)
LOUISIANA-STYLE EGGPLANT
COMPOTE AMULET
MELROSE PUDDING

Serves 6 to 8

BASS À LA BRIN

2 (2½-pound) whole bass, cleaned
½ cup all-purpose flour
Salt and pepper to taste
6 cups boiling water
1 cup vinegar
2 teaspoons salt
2 medium onions, sliced
24 peppercorns
⅛ teaspoon ground mace
¼ cup butter or margarine
¼ cup all-purpose flour
2 tablespoons lemon juice
¼ teaspoon salt
⅛ teaspoon pepper
Chopped fresh parsley
Lemon slices

Wash fish well; place in salted water to cover for 30 minutes. Drain. Pat fish dry; dredge in flour, and sprinkle with salt and pepper. Wrap fish in cheesecloth, and tie ends securely.

Combine water, vinegar, 2 teaspoons salt, onion, peppercorns, and mace in a large Dutch oven; stir well. Add fish; simmer, uncovered, over low heat 30 minutes. Drain, reserving 1 cup fish stock. Set fish aside, and keep warm.

Combine butter and flour in a medium saucepan, stirring until lightly browned. Stir in reserved fish stock, lemon juice, salt, and pepper, blending until smooth. Remove fish from cheesecloth; place on a large serving platter, and pour sauce over top. Sprinkle with parsley, and garnish with lemon slices. Yield: 8 servings.

Shreveport

Natchitoches

POTATO MARRAINE

4 medium potatoes, peeled
1 teaspoon salt, divided
¼ cup butter or margarine, softened
1 cup hot milk
¼ teaspoon pepper
1 egg, beaten
Fresh parsley sprigs

Place potatoes in saucepan; add ½ teaspoon salt and water to cover. Set aside for 1 hour.

Cook potatoes over medium heat for 30 minutes or until tender. Remove from pan; mash, and beat well with electric mixer until potatoes are smooth.

Combine butter, milk, remaining salt, and pepper; add to potatoes, stirring well. While mixture is warm, shape into 24 oval potato puffs, using about ¼ cup of mixture for each puff. Place on a greased cookie sheet, and brush each potato puff with egg. Bake at 425° for 15 minutes or until lightly browned. Garnish with parsley. Yield: 2 dozen.

Bass à la Brin served with Rice Croquettes.

RIZ ISLE BREVELLE

2½ cups water
¾ cup uncooked regular rice
¾ teaspoon salt
1½ cups tomato juice
1½ tablespoons sugar
½ teaspoon salt
⅛ teaspoon pepper
1½ tablespoons butter or
  margarine
1½ teaspoons onion juice
5 egg yolks, beaten
3 tablespoons grated
  Parmesan cheese
2 egg yolks
1½ tablespoons milk
About 1½ cups cracker
  crumbs
Vegetable oil

Bring water to a boil in a large saucepan; add rice and salt. Boil 10 minutes; drain.

Combine next 4 ingredients; stir into rice. Cook over low heat 10 minutes. Remove from heat; add butter and onion juice. Stir in 5 egg yolks and cheese, mixing well. Cook over low heat 3 minutes. Remove from heat; cool. Shape into croquettes.

Combine 2 egg yolks and milk, beating well. Dip croquettes into egg mixture; dredge in cracker crumbs, coating well.

Chill croquettes 1 hour. Fry in 1 inch of hot oil (375°) until golden brown. Drain on paper towels. Yield: 9 croquettes.

Pounding rice grown in Louisiana.

LOUISIANA-STYLE EGGPLANT

1 small eggplant
4 medium tomatoes, sliced
2 medium-size green peppers,
  chopped
2 medium onions, chopped
¾ teaspoon salt
¼ teaspoon pepper
⅛ teaspoon garlic powder
1 (12-ounce) package sharp
  Cheddar cheese, cut into
  ⅛-inch slices

Cut eggplant into ¼-inch slices; cook in a small amount of boiling water for 5 to 10 minutes or until eggplant is tender. Drain well.

Place eggplant in a lightly greased 13- x 9- x 2-inch baking dish. Place tomato slices on top of eggplant. Combine green pepper, onion, salt, pepper, and garlic powder; sprinkle evenly over tomato slices. Cover and bake at 400° for 20 minutes; reduce heat to 350° and bake, uncovered, an additional 35 minutes.

Arrange cheese slices on top during last 10 minutes of baking time. Yield: 6 to 8 servings.

25

COMPOTE AMULET

6 oranges, peeled and
  sectioned
¾ cup grated coconut
1½ cups chopped pecans
1 (11-ounce) can mandarin
  oranges, undrained
Lettuce leaves
⅔ cup mayonnaise
3 maraschino cherries,
  chopped

Combine first 4 ingredients.
Toss; chill. Spoon onto lettuce
leaves. Spread mayonnaise over
fruit; garnish with cherries.
Yield: 6 to 8 servings.

MELROSE PUDDING

2 cups fine, dry breadcrumbs,
  divided
½ cup milk
1 tablespoon butter, softened
¾ cup sugar
6 eggs, separated
2 teaspoons grated lemon
  rind
3 tablespoons lemon juice
1 (8-ounce) package coconut
  macaroons
¾ cup sherry, divided
1 cup apple jelly
½ pound sponge cake, cut
  into ½-inch slices

Combine 1 cup breadcrumbs
and milk; stir well. Set aside.

Cream butter; gradually add
sugar, beating well. Add egg
yolks, one at a time, beating well
after each addition. Add breadcrumb mixture, lemon rind,
and juice; mix well.

Beat egg whites (at room temperature) until stiff peaks form.
Fold whites into yolk mixture.

Cover bottom of a greased 2-
quart casserole with a thin layer
of custard mixture. Layer macaroons evenly over custard;
sprinkle with ¼ cup sherry.
Pour one-half of remaining custard mixture over macaroons.

Spread jelly on cake slices.
Place slices over custard layer.
Sprinkle remaining bread-
crumbs over top. Add remaining
sherry; top with remaining custard. Cover; bake at 350° for 35
minutes or until set. Serve
warm. Yield: 6 to 8 servings.

B.A. Cohen

C lementine Hunter put the Melrose Plantation House (above) on the epicurean map with game soup, parsnip fritters, and apple biscuits. Also an artist, her early paintings, left and right, were crude, but national recognition came after her first show in New Orleans in 1950.

NEW ORLEANS CREOLE DINNER

What follows is an abbreviated version of the dinner that the New Orleans Press Club sat down to back in 1898. Absinthe was on that menu and the delegates were aware of its effects, " . . . derangement of the digestive organs, delirium, and idiocy." Modern media critics should be aware that the bitter green liqueur is no longer available in such lethal form. We have substituted Sazerac cocktails and Ramos Gin Fizzes. For the Press Club's

"Small Creole Dinner," Steward George G. Voitier composed a menu that was a model of good humor, interspersing between the dishes such Creole wisdom as "Don't tie your dogs with sausages."

About the "Gombo filé" (to be served with "Small vegetables with salt"), he said:

With a good gombo prepared
by Silvie,
Without ever scolding I would
pass my life.

SAZERAC COCKTAIL
RAMOS GIN FIZZ
CREOLE CANAPÉS
BROILED OYSTERS
RED BEANS AND RICE
GUMBO FILÉ
ASSORTED SMALL VEGETABLES WITH SALT
SWEET POTATO BREAD
SUGARED PECANS

Serves 8 to 10

SAZERAC COCKTAIL

¼ teaspoon Simple Syrup
1¼ ounces bourbon whiskey
⅛ teaspoon angostura bitters
½ teaspoon anisette
Lemon twist

Combine first 3 ingredients, blending well. Set aside.

Pour anisette into a chilled old-fashioned glass. Tilt glass to coat well. Discard anisette.

Strain bourbon mixture; pour into glass. Serve garnishd with lemon twist. Yield: 1 serving.

Simple Syrup:

1 cup sugar
1 cup water

Combine all ingredients in a heavy saucepan; cook over medium heat for 1 minute until sugar is dissolved, stirring constantly. Yield: about 1 cup.

Note: Simple Syrup may be stored in an airtight glass container in the refrigerator.

RAMOS GIN FIZZ

2 teaspoons super-fine
granulated sugar
1 egg white
¼ teaspoon orange flower
water
¼ cup milk
1½ tablespoons lemon juice
⅛ teaspoon vanilla extract
1 ounce gin
Crushed ice

Combine first 7 ingredients in container of an electric blender; process well. Pour over crushed ice in prepared glass. Yield: 1 serving.

Creole Canapés served with Ramos Gin Fizz, originated by the colorful bartender at the Roosevelt Hotel in New Orleans, and Sazerac Cocktail, named for a New Orleans hero.

CREOLE CANAPÉS

1 cup minced lean ham
1 medium onion, finely chopped
1 clove garlic, minced
1 tablespoon butter or margarine
1 medium tomato, peeled, seeded, and finely chopped
1 medium-size green pepper, finely chopped
½ teaspoon salt
⅛ teaspoon pepper
Dash of red pepper
8 slices bread
2 tablespoons butter or margarine, melted
¼ cup grated Parmesan cheese

Sauté ham, onion, and garlic in 1 tablespoon butter in a large skillet for 3 minutes. Add tomato, green pepper, salt, and pepper; cook over medium heat for 15 minutes or until liquid is absorbed.

Remove crust from each slice of bread, and cut each slice into 1- x 3-inch strips. Brush bread strips with melted butter. Place on ungreased baking sheet, and lightly toast.

Spread ham mixture over bread strips; sprinkle with cheese. Bake at 350° for 5 minutes. Serve hot. Yield: about 1½ dozen.

BROILED OYSTERS

3 (12-ounce) cans fresh Select oysters, drained
¼ teaspoon salt
⅛ teaspoon red pepper
Lemon slices
½ cup butter or margarine, melted

Place oysters in a 13- x 9- x 2-inch baking dish. Sprinkle with salt and pepper. Broil 4 inches from heat 5 minutes or until oysters are curled. Turn, and broil 5 minutes or until lightly browned. Remove from baking dish; drain well. Place on warm serving platter; garnish with lemon slices. Serve with melted butter. Yield: 8 to 10 servings.

RED BEANS AND RICE

2 pounds dried red beans
1 pound salt pork, cut into 1-inch cubes
1 cup chopped onion
½ cup chopped carrot
½ cup chopped celery
2 tablespoons vinegar
2 bay leaves
1 teaspoon salt
½ teaspoon pepper
Hot cooked rice
Hot sauce

Sort and wash beans; place in a large Dutch oven. Cover with water 2 inches above beans; let soak overnight. Drain beans; cover with water, and bring to a boil. Add next 6 ingredients; stir gently.

Reduce heat; cover, and simmer 2 to 2½ hours or until beans are tender and a thick gravy is formed. Add water to prevent beans from sticking, if necessary. Stir in salt and pepper. Serve with rice and hot sauce. Yield: 8 to 10 servings.

GUMBO FILÉ

½ teaspoon salt
½ teaspoon pepper
1 (2½- to 3-pound)
   broiler-fryer, cut up
¾ cup country ham, diced
2 tablespoons butter or
   margarine, melted
2 (12-ounce) cans fresh
   oysters, undrained
1 large onion, chopped
½ teaspoon chopped fresh
   parsley
1 bay leaf
½ whole red pepper pod
¼ teaspoon salt
¼ teaspoon ground red
   pepper
¼ teaspoon ground thyme
¼ teaspoon pepper
Hot cooked rice
Gumbo filé (optional)

Sprinkle salt and pepper over chicken pieces. Brown chicken and ham in butter in a large Dutch oven. Set aside.

Drain oysters; add water to oyster liquid to measure 2 quarts. Refrigerate oysters.

Combine oyster water and next 8 ingredients, stirring well; add to Dutch oven. Simmer 1½ hours or until chicken is tender.

Remove chicken from broth; bone, and cut into bite-size pieces. Return chicken to broth. Cool; cover and refrigerate overnight.

Skim fat from cold gumbo, and bring to a boil; reduce heat, and add oysters. Heat thoroughly and serve over rice. Add a small amount of filé to each serving, if a thicker gumbo is desired. Yield: about 3 quarts.

SWEET POTATO BREAD

2 packages dry yeast
½ cup warm water (105°
   to 115°)
7 cups all-purpose flour
1½ tablespoons firmly packed
   brown sugar
1 tablespoon salt
¼ teaspoon ground cinnamon
¼ teaspoon ground nutmeg
⅛ teaspoon white pepper
1 cup warm water (105°
   to 115°), divided
2 cups cooked, mashed sweet
   potatoes
2 tablespoons butter, melted

Dissolve yeast in ½ cup warm water in large mixing bowl, and set aside.

Combine flour, brown sugar, salt, and spices. Add ½ cup flour mixture to yeast mixture, stirring well. Gradually add an additional ½ cup flour mixture and ¼ cup warm water to yeast mixture; stir well. Repeat procedure with warm water and 5 cups flour mixture, reserving remaining flour mixture. Stir in sweet potatoes and butter (dough will be sticky).

Turn dough out onto a lightly floured surface; knead, adding reserved 1 cup flour mixture, 1 tablespoon at a time. Knead for 10 to 15 minutes or until dough is smooth and elastic.

Place dough in a greased bowl, turning to grease top. Cover, and let rise in a warm place (85°), free from drafts, for 1 hour or until doubled in bulk.

Punch dough down, and divide in half; shape each into a loaf. Place in two well-greased 9- x 5- x 3-inch loafpans. Cover, and let rise in a warm place (85°), free from drafts, for 30 minutes or until doubled in bulk. Bake at 425° for 30 minutes or until loaves sound hollow when tapped. Yield: 2 loaves.

Colorfully dressed Choctaw women selling their home-grown herbs at the New Orleans market.

Léon J. Frémaux, *Characters of New Orleans*, 1876

SUGARED PECANS

½ cup butter or margarine
2 egg whites
1 cup sugar
Dash of salt
3 cups pecan halves

Melt butter in a 13- x 9- x 2-inch baking pan.

Beat egg whites (at room temperature) until soft peaks form; gradually add sugar and salt, beating until very stiff. Fold in pecans. Spread pecan mixture in prepared pan. Bake at 325° for 30 to 35 minutes or until mixture is browned and all butter is absorbed, stirring at 10 minute intervals to coat evenly. Remove to waxed paper while still warm; cool completely. Store pecans in an airtight container. Yield: about 3½ cups.

Interior of New Orleans' famous French Market, c. 1895, where goods offered for sale included seafood, sugar cane, and fresh strawberries.

SOUTHWESTERN INDIAN FARE

The Eastern Indian tribes were accustomed to baking flat corn "platter bread" on hot stones oiled with animal fat or nut oil. It was not until the early 1800s, when the United States government resettled these tribes in Oklahoma, that "fry bread" came into being. The uprooted Indians were given rations of beef during the westward trek and wheat flour, not corn. Flour, cooking utensils, and dire necessity resulted in fry bread. With leavening added later on, the mixture differs little from biscuit dough. Once re-established, the Indians planted corn again.

BEEF STEW
WILTED WATERCRESS SALAD
INDIAN FRY BREAD
CORN PONE
FRESH BLACKBERRIES OR HUCKLEBERRIES
WITH CREAM
SASSAFRAS TEA

Serves 6 to 8

BEEF STEW

2½ pounds lean boneless chuck steak, trimmed and cut into 1-inch cubes
½ cup all-purpose flour
Vegetable oil
3 medium onions, chopped
3 large carrots, scraped and cut into 2-inch pieces
3 medium potatoes, peeled and cubed
2 stalks celery, cut into 1-inch pieces
1 (17-ounce) can whole kernel corn, drained
1 (28-ounce) can whole tomatoes, undrained
1 clove garlic, minced
1½ teaspoons salt
1 teaspoon pepper
¼ teaspoon ground oregano
1½ cups water

Dredge meat in flour, and brown in small amount of vegetable oil in an 8-quart Dutch oven. Add remaining ingredients; cover, and simmer 2½ hours or until vegetables are tender. Yield 8 servings.

Beef Stew: A hearty meal of beef and vegetables cooked over an open fire.

Photograph by Laura Gilpin. © Amon Carter Museum, Fort Worth.

I ate this at our county fair.

Making fry bread at Blessingway, Crownpoint.

WILTED WATERCRESS SALAD

6 cups watercress
6 slices bacon
5 to 6 radishes (optional)

Place watercress in a salad bowl. Cook bacon in a large skillet until crisp; remove bacon, reserving drippings. Crumble bacon, and set aside.

Pour bacon drippings over watercress. Toss gently. Sprinkle with bacon before serving. Garnish with radishes, if desired. Yield: 6 to 8 servings.

Note: 6 cups leaf lettuce may be substituted for watercress.

INDIAN FRY BREAD

1½ cups all-purpose flour
2 teaspoons baking powder
½ teaspoon salt
¾ cup milk
Honey

Combine dry ingredients; add milk, and stir until mixture forms a ball.

Roll out onto a lightly floured surface to ⅛-inch thickness; cut into rectangles 1 inch wide and 3 inches long.

Gently place dough rectangles in ½ inch of hot oil (375°), a few at a time, lightly pressing down with the back of a fork until dough becomes firm. Turn, and cook on other side until golden in color. Drain; serve immediately with honey. Yield: about 2½ dozen.

CORN PONE

1 cup yellow cornmeal
½ cup all-purpose flour
2 teaspoons baking powder
1 tablespoon sugar
½ teaspoon salt
1 cup milk

Combine all ingredients, mixing well. Drop batter by teaspoonfuls into deep hot oil (375°); fry only a few at a time, turning once. Cook 3 to 5 minutes or until golden brown. Drain on paper towels. Yield: about 3½ dozen.

SASSAFRAS TEA

6 (2-inch) sassafras roots
6 cups water

Combine sassafras and water in a large saucepan; bring to a boil. Remove from heat; cover, and steep for 15 minutes. Strain tea. Yield: 6 cups.

FROM SOUTH OF THE BORDER

exas was not a part of Mexico for over three hundred years for nothing. Mexican food is an integral part of the Texas that emerged from the defeat of Santa Anna by Sam Houston in 1836. At that time the Mexicans in Texas were eating "tortilla, beef, venison, chicken, eggs, cheese, and milk," according to a contemporary statistical report. Beans and tortillas, however, have traditionally formed the backbone of the Mexican diet. Chiles, cumin, coriander, garlic, and onions are a few flavorful hallmarks of one of the most interesting of Southern cuisines.

GUACAMOLE DIP WITH
FRIED TORTILLA CHIPS
BLACK BEAN SOUP
GREEN ENCHILADAS
TAMALES
SOPA DE ARROZ (Mexican Rice)
EMPANADAS DULCES (Sweet Potato Pies)
MEXICAN BEER or SANGRÍA

Serves 6

Sangría, Guacamole Dip, and Fried Tortilla Chips.

GUACAMOLE DIP

2 medium avocados, peeled and mashed
1 medium tomato, peeled and finely chopped
1 small onion, minced
1 clove garlic, crushed
2 tablespoons vinegar
½ teaspoon olive oil
Leaf lettuce
Tomato wedges

Combine first 6 ingredients; mix well. Cover, and chill thoroughly. Arrange on lettuce leaves, and garnish with tomato wedges. Serve with tortilla chips. Yield: about 2½ cups.

FRIED TORTILLA CHIPS

1 dozen frozen corn tortillas, thawed
Vegetable oil

Cut each tortilla into 4 pieces. Fry in hot oil (375°) in a large skillet until golden brown. Drain on paper towels. Yield: 4 dozen chips.

West Side of the Main Plaza, San Antonio, Texas, 1849, by W.G.M. Samuel.

BLACK BEAN SOUP

1 pound dried black beans
2 quarts water
1 medium onion, chopped
1 teaspoon salt
1 teaspoon pepper
1 tablespoon butter or
  margarine
½ teaspoon lemon juice
½ teaspoon prepared mustard

Sort and wash beans. Place in a large Dutch oven, and cover with water 2 inches above beans; let soak overnight. Drain beans, and return to Dutch oven; add water and onion. Bring to a boil. Reduce heat; cover, and simmer 2 to 3 hours or until tender, adding more water if necessary.

Process beans in electric blender until smooth. Return mixture to Dutch oven; stir in remaining ingredients. Cook over low heat, stirring frequently, until thoroughly heated. Yield: about 4 cups.

GREEN ENCHILADAS

16 corn tortillas
Vegetable oil
Green Sauce
5 cups (20 ounces)
  shredded Cheddar cheese,
  divided
1 cup chopped onion

Heat ¼-inch vegetable oil in a large skillet until oil is hot. Cook tortillas, one at a time, 5 seconds on each side or until softened. Drain tortillas thoroughly on paper towels; dip each tortilla in Green Sauce.

Sprinkle about 3 cups cheese evenly over tortillas. Sprinkle onion over cheese.

Roll up each tortilla; place seam side down in 2 lightly greased 13- x 9- x 2-inch baking dishes. Pour remaining Green Sauce over top; sprinkle with remaining cheese.

Bake enchiladas at 350° for 20 minutes. Serve immediately. Yield: 6 to 8 servings.

Green Sauce:

4 medium-size green
  tomatoes, peeled
4 medium-size green peppers,
  cut into fourths
1 cup chopped onion
3 cups water
¼ cup plus 3 tablespoons
  all-purpose flour
¼ cup vegetable oil
1½ cloves garlic, crushed

Combine tomatoes, peppers, onion, and water in a large Dutch oven; cook over medium heat about 30 minutes or until vegetables are tender.

Place vegetables and liquid in container of electric blender; set on high speed, and process until smooth.

Combine flour, oil, and garlic in a medium saucepan; cook over low heat, stirring constantly, until mixture is lightly browned. Add vegetable mixture; cook over low heat 15 minutes, stirring occasionally. Yield: about 4 cups.

Marketplace at Smiler, Texas, c. 1887.

TAMALES

1½ pounds boneless chuck
  roast
½ pound boneless lean pork
1 tablespoon vinegar
1 teaspoon salt
½ teaspoon pepper
4 cups water
2 to 3 dozen dried corn husks
2 cloves garlic, crushed
1 tablespoon cumin seeds
3 tablespoons shortening,
  melted
1 tablespoon chili powder
1½ teaspoons salt
½ teaspoon pepper
2 cups plus 2 tablespoons
  instant corn masa
1½ teaspoons chili powder
¾ teaspoon salt
1½ tablespoons shortening,
  melted

Combine beef, pork, vinegar, 1 teaspoon salt, ½ teaspoon pepper, and water in a Dutch oven; cook over low heat about 2½ hours or until meat is tender. Drain, reserving liquid. Shred meat with a fork.

Cover dried corn husks with hot water; let stand 1 to 2 hours or until softened. Drain well, and pat with paper towels to remove excess water. (If husks are too narrow, overlap 2 husks to make a wide one. If husks are too wide, tear off one side.) Use an 8- x 8-inch aluminum foil square for each tamale if dried corn husks are not available.

Sauté garlic and cumin seeds in 3 tablespoons shortening for 5 minutes. Add shredded meat, 1 cup reserved meat broth, 1 tablespoon chili powder, 1½ tea-

spoons salt, and ½ teaspoon pepper. Cook, uncovered, over low heat 30 minutes, stirring occasionally.

Combine corn masa, 1½ teaspoons chili powder, and ¾ teaspoon salt in a large mixing bowl; stir well. Add 1¼ cups reserved meat broth and 1½ table-

SOPA DE ARROZ

2 tablespoons shortening
1 cup uncooked regular rice
1 small onion, chopped
1 small green pepper, chopped
1 clove garlic, minced
2 large tomatoes, peeled and chopped
2 cups water
1 teaspoon salt
¼ teaspoon pepper

Combine shortening and rice in a large skillet. Cook over medium heat until lightly browned.

Add onion, green pepper, and garlic; cook, stirring constantly, until tender. Add tomatoes, water, salt, and pepper; cover, and cook over low heat for 20 minutes. Serve immediately. Yield: 6 servings.

EMPANADAS DULCES

1 (17-ounce) can yams
1 (15¼-ounce) can crushed pineapple, undrained
1 cup plus 3 tablespoons sugar, divided
1½ teaspoons lemon rind
1½ teaspoons orange rind
2½ cups all-purpose flour
1 teaspoon baking powder
½ teaspoon salt
¾ cup shortening
5 to 6 tablespoons cold water
Additional sugar

Combine yams, pineapple, 1 cup sugar, lemon and orange rind in a large saucepan. Cook over medium heat, stirring constantly, until thickened. Cool; set aside.

Combine flour, remaining 3 tablespoons sugar, baking powder, and salt; cut in shortening with pastry blender until mixture resembles coarse meal. Sprinkle cold water evenly over surface; stir with a fork until all ingredients are moistened. Divide pastry into 22 to 24 portions. Roll each portion to a 3-inch circle on a lightly floured surface.

Place about 1 tablespoon pineapple mixture on each pastry circle. Moisten edges of circle; fold pastry in half, making sure edges are even.

Using a fork dipped in flour, press edges of pastry together to seal. Sprinkle ½ teaspoon sugar on each pastry. Place on baking sheets; bake at 350° for 30 minutes or until lightly browned. Yield: about 2 dozen.

spoons shortening; mix the dough well.

Place 1 tablespoon of dough in the center of each husk; spread to within ½ inch of edge. Place 1 tablespoon meat mixture on dough, spreading evenly. Fold sides of husk to center, enclosing filling completely. Fold pointed end under; tie with string or narrow strips of softened corn husk.

Place a coffee cup in the center of a rack in a large pot. Add just enough water to fill pot below rack level in order to keep tamales above water.

Stand tamales on folded ends around the cup. Bring water to a boil. Cover, and steam 1½ hours or until dough pulls away from husk, adding water as needed. Yield: 1½ dozen.

SANGRÍA

6 oranges, thinly sliced
3 lemons, thinly sliced
1 lime, thinly sliced
1½ cups sugar
1 cup brandy
1 gallon Burgandy or other dry red wine

Arrange orange, lemon and lime slices in bottom of a large punch bowl; sprinkle with sugar. Pour brandy over fruit; cover, and let stand at least 1 hour. Add wine; mix well. Let stand at least 1 hour. Serve over ice. Yield: about 1 gallon.

TEXAS HILL COUNTRY BARBECUE

Expect beef to be the center of attraction when an invitation comes in for a Texas Hill Country barbecue, for that is the staff of life in those parts. There may be some ribs and chicken as well, but not necessarily. Texas' famous smoked sausage turns up almost every time. The barbecue sauce used by Texans may be more correctly defined as a mopping sauce used in cooking to flavor and moisten the meat. It usually does not even taste good, so any favorite barbecue sauce can be served with the meat, if desired. However, purists prefer just the smoked flavor.

BARBECUE SAUCE * BARBECUED RIBS
BARBECUED BRISKET * BARBECUED SAUSAGE
TEXAS COLESLAW * DILL PICKLES
RANCH-STYLE PINTO BEANS
HOT POTATO SALAD
SOURDOUGH BISCUITS
FRIED APPLE PIES

Serves 12

BARBECUE SAUCE

1½ cups shortening, melted
1 clove garlic, minced
Dash of pepper
1 small lemon, thinly sliced
½ medium onion, finely
  chopped
1 teaspoon chili powder
2 cups vinegar
½ cup red wine vinegar

Combine all ingredients in a saucepan; bring to a boil. Cook over medium heat 5 minutes. Use warm as a basting sauce. Yield: about 4½ cups.

BARBECUED RIBS

12 pounds spareribs
Hot water
Barbecue Sauce
  (see left)

Place ribs in a large Dutch oven; add water to cover. Cover, and simmer over medium heat 30 minutes. Remove from pan; drain well.

Prepare charcoal fire in a smoker, and let burn 10 to 15 minutes. Place food rack in smoker. Place ribs on rack; baste with Barbecue Sauce.

Grill ribs over medium coals for 3 minutes on each side. Remove rack and meat from smoker.

Place water pan in smoker, filling with water. Place rack and meat in smoker. Cover, and cook over low coals for 2 hours. Remove waterpan from smoker. Replace rack and meat. Baste with Barbecue Sauce; cover, and cook for 1 hour or until desired degree of doneness, turning meat and basting with Barbecue Sauce every 10 minutes. Yield: 12 servings.

BARBECUED BRISKET

1 (4- to 6-pound) boneless
  beef brisket
½ gallon vinegar
2 cups hickory chips
Hot water
Barbecue Sauce (see above)

Place meat in a large container, and pour vinegar over it. Cover; chill 4 to 6 hours.

Soak 2 cups hickory chips in water to cover; set aside.

Prepare charcoal fire in a smoker, and let burn 10 to 15 minutes. Drain meat well. Place food rack in smoker. Place meat on rack; grill over medium coals 4 to 5 minutes on each side or until browned. Remove rack and meat from smoker.

Drain hickory chips, and add to charcoal in smoker. Place water pan in smoker, and fill with water. Place rack and meat, fat side down, in smoker. Cover, and cook over low coals about 5 hours.

Remove waterpan from smoker. Replace rack and meat; baste meat with Barbecue Sauce. Cover, and cook for 1 hour or until desired degree of doneness, turning meat and basting with Barbecue Sauce every 10 minutes. Cut thin slices diagonally across the grain. Yield: 12 to 15 servings.

Texas Hill Barbecue complete with accompaniments.

City meat market, Midland, Texas, 1895.

BARBECUED SAUSAGE

2 pounds smoked sausage
1½ cups Barbecue Sauce
  (page 38)

Place sausage on grill over low coals. Grill about 15 minutes; turn sausage, and baste with Barbecue Sauce. Continue cooking for 1 hour and 15 minutes, turning and basting sausage every 15 minutes. Cut into 1-inch slices to serve. Yield: 12 servings.

TEXAS COLESLAW

2 (6-ounce) cans evaporated
  milk
¼ cup sugar
1 teaspoon salt
½ teaspoon pepper
¼ cup vinegar
6 cups finely shredded
  cabbage

Combine first 4 ingredients; mix well. Gradually add vinegar, stirring constantly; cover, and chill at least 1 hour.

Pour dressing over cabbage; mix well. Cover, and chill at least 1 hour. Yield: 12 servings.

RANCH-STYLE PINTO BEANS

1½ pounds dried pinto beans
1 medium onion, chopped
1½ cloves garlic, minced
3 tablespoons chili powder
2 teaspoons salt
⅛ teaspoon pepper

Sort and wash beans; place in a large Dutch oven. Add water to cover 2 inches above beans; soak overnight. Drain beans; add water to cover. Add remaining ingredients; stir well.

Cover, and bring to a boil; reduce heat. Simmer two hours or until beans are tender, stirring occasionally. Add water, if necessary, to prevent beans from sticking. Yield: 12 servings.

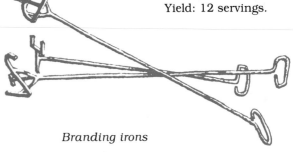

Branding irons

HOT POTATO SALAD

12 medium potatoes
12 slices bacon
2 large onions, finely chopped
1 tablespoon salt
½ teaspoon pepper
1 cup vinegar

Scrub potatoes; cook in boiling water for 30 minutes or until tender. Drain, and cool slightly. Peel potatoes, and cut into ¾-inch cubes; set aside.

Cook bacon in a large skillet until crisp; remove bacon, reserving drippings in skillet. Crumble bacon, and set aside.

Sauté onion in pan drippings until tender. Stir in salt, pepper, and vinegar; bring mixture to a boil. Remove mixture from heat; add reserved bacon, mixing well. Pour mixture over potatoes; mix well, and serve hot. Yield: 12 servings.

SOURDOUGH BISCUITS

4 cups all-purpose flour
1 tablespoon sugar
1½ teaspoons baking powder
1 teaspoon salt
½ teaspoon baking soda
2 tablespoons shortening
2½ cups Sourdough Starter at room temperature
Melted butter

Combine first 5 ingredients in a nonmetal bowl; mix well. Cut in 2 tablespoons shortening until mixture resembles coarse meal. Add Sourdough Starter, stirring until moistened. Turn dough out onto a lightly floured surface, and knead lightly 3 or 4 times.

Roll dough out to ½-inch thickness; cut with a 2½-inch biscuit cutter. Place biscuits in 3 lightly greased 9-inch square baking pans, and brush tops with melted butter. Cover, and let rise in a warm place (85°), free from drafts, 45 minutes or until doubled in bulk. Bake at 450° for 10 to 12 minutes or until lightly browned. Yield: about 3 dozen.

Sourdough Starter:

1 package dry yeast
4 cups warm water (105° to 115°)
2 cups buttermilk
2 cups all-purpose flour
2 tablespoons instant mashed potatoes
1 tablespoon sugar

Dissolve yeast in warm water; let stand 5 minutes. Combine buttermilk, flour, mashed potatoes, and sugar in a medium-size nonmetal bowl; mix well. Add yeast mixture, and stir until well combined.

Cover loosely with plastic wrap or cheesecloth, and let stand in a warm place (80° to 85°) for 12 hours.

To use, stir well, and measure amount of starter needed for recipe. Replenish remaining starter with 3 parts flour to 2 parts water and 1 teaspoon sugar. For example, if 1½ cups starter is used, add 1½ cups flour, 1 cup warm water (105° to 115°), and 1 teaspoon sugar. Stir until blended.

Stir in 1 teaspoon sugar daily when not used to keep starter active. Yield: 6 cups.

Photograph taken in 1898 captures cowboys taking time out on the trail for a meal—with sourdough biscuits, no doubt!

FRIED APPLE PIES

1 (8-ounce) package dried
  apples
1 cup water
2 tablespoons butter or
  margarine, melted
¾ cup sugar
1 teaspoon ground cinnamon
¼ teaspoon ground nutmeg
2 tablespoons lemon juice
Pastry (recipe follows)
Vegetable oil

Soak apples overnight in water to cover; drain, and rinse well. Combine apples and 1 cup water in a large saucepan; bring to a boil. Reduce heat; cover, and simmer 30 minutes or until tender. Cool. Stir in butter, sugar, cinnamon, nutmeg, and lemon juice; mash well.

Divide pastry into thirds; roll each portion to ⅛-inch thickness on waxed paper. Cut into 4-inch circles.

Place about 1 tablespoon apple mixture on half of each pastry circle. Dip fingers in water, and moisten edges of circles; fold in half, making sure edges are even. Press pastry edges firmly together using a fork dipped in flour.

Heat 1 inch of oil to 375° in a large skillet. Cook pies until golden brown on both sides, turning once. Drain well on paper towels. Yield: 2 dozen.

Pastry:

4 cups all-purpose flour
2 teaspoons baking powder
1 teaspoon salt
1 cup butter or margarine
¾ to 1 cup cold water

Combine first 3 ingredients; cut in butter until mixture resembles coarse meal. Sprinkle water over flour mixture; stir with a fork until dry ingredients are moistened. Shape dough into a ball, and wrap in waxed paper; chill at least 1 hour or until ready to use. Yield: enough pastry for 2 dozen 4-inch pies.

Clara Irene McDonald Williamson was born in Bosque County, Texas, in 1875. Frontier life allowed no leisure time; "Aunt Clara" did not turn to painting until she was widowed in her late sixties. Her work is classified as primitive or naive. It glows with a depth of feeling and spontaneity, and reflects her rich retentive memory; she painted from her heart and mind. Hers are mind pictures of cattle drives and scenes and people of her little town of Iredell. Her style did not evolve; her first artistic expression was to remain her personal art form.

Get Along Little Dogies *by Clara Irene McDonald Williamson.*

SEASONAL SPECIALTIES

Nature's Bounties in the Southland

The Creoles used to say that "Nature itself tells us what to eat." True enough, before railroad shipment of Deep South produce northward became possible after the Civil War. Now, thanks to refrigerated freighting, springtime is more a state of mind than of weather when it comes to menu planning. The supermarket and the home deep freeze have replaced Nature in telling us what to eat.

In the tropic South, with two full growing seasons, there is scarcely a month during which a home garden is not producing something fresh for the table. So Mother Nature can still tell the Creoles to eat open-ground grown cucumbers in late April, even while saying to the gardener in the Upper South, "Hang in there; don't plant until after the last frost." What we can do, of course, is slog through snow to the "super" and have wilted lettuce and green onions in January, if we please. In measuring such progress, we might balance off gains against certain losses: memories of what seasons used to mean.

In a lyrical piece based on her childhood memories of southern Alabama, Celestine Sibley wrote of the "Aprilness" of a day when "My mother came up from the garden with a basket of young mustard greens and onions. 'Come help me wash them,' she invited. 'We'll have them wilted with bacon drippings for supper.' The first of the season!"

A boy away at school in Virginia, in a letter dated May 20, 1861, wrote, ". . . The strawberries are beginning to ripen quite fast. I am tolerably well contented to stay here with a plenty of them to eat. . . ."

And this memory by Evelyn P. Baer of a 1920s visit to Cownes plantation in Virginia: ". . . Emma led us on endless walks through the woods. . . . The sun-ripened blackberries growing wild along the hedgerows had a delicate perfume and seemed the very flavor of summer."

Here was once the significance of fall, according to the diaries kept by Kentucky's Shakers: "September 4, 1848: Began to dry punkin." "September 22, 1845: Commenced cutting and drying apples." Winter, the first really cold part, has always been hog-killing time. "November 17, 1841: The Office hogs was killed."

A SPRING CELEBRATION SUPPER

Anytime we find fresh asparagus and raspberries in the market or in the home garden, it is cause to celebrate. About that same time, the parsley from last year's crop begins to show a few volunteer leaves, and tiny new potatoes are ready to be "scrabbled" out of the ground. Whatever else is in the menu, it will sing "Spring." Years ago, chickens ran about the barnlot while the cook kept an educated eye on them, awaiting the day when she could legally call the feisty critters "spring chickens" and put them on the dinner table. Tell a youngster his grandmother is as spry as a spring chicken and try to explain your way out of *that!*

TOMATO ASPIC
LEMON-ROASTED CHICKEN
FRESH ASPARAGUS
NEW POTATOES WITH PARSLEY BUTTER
CHEESE BISCUITS
RASPBERRY FOOL

Serves 4

TOMATO ASPIC

1 package unflavored gelatin
¼ cup cold water
2 cups tomato juice
1 medium onion, sliced
½ cup sliced celery
1 teaspoon tarragon vinegar
3 whole peppercorns
2 whole bay leaves
¼ teaspoon salt
Leaf lettuce
Mayonnaise
Paprika

Soften gelatin in water, and set aside.

Combine tomato juice and next 6 ingredients in a large saucepan; bring to a boil. Reduce heat, and simmer 10 minutes. Strain tomato juice mixture; add gelatin, stirring until dissolved. Pour into 4 lightly oiled ½-cup molds; chill until mixture is firm.

Unmold on a lettuce-lined serving plate. Garnish with a dollop of mayonnaise; sprinkle with paprika. Yield: 4 servings.

LEMON-ROASTED CHICKEN

1 (3- to 3½-pound) broiler-fryer
¼ cup butter or margarine
4 cups chicken broth, undiluted
3 tablespoons lemon juice
1 large lemon, sliced (optional)
Fresh parsley sprigs (optional)

Rinse chicken and pat dry. Rub outside of chicken lightly with 3 tablespoons butter. Place remaining butter in cavity of chicken, and truss securely.

Place chicken, breast side up, in a shallow roasting pan. Combine chicken broth and lemon juice; pour over chicken. Bake at 400°, basting occasionally, for 1 hour and 10 minutes or until done. Garnish with lemon slices and parsley, if desired. Yield: 4 servings.

FRESH ASPARAGUS

1½ pounds fresh asparagus spears
3 tablespoons butter or margarine
¼ teaspoon salt
⅛ teaspoon pepper
Pimiento strips (optional)

Wash asparagus; snap off tough ends. Remove scales with a knife or vegetable peeler.

Place asparagus in layers in a lightly greased 1-quart casserole; dot with butter, and sprinkle with salt and pepper.

Cover and bake at 300° for 35 to 40 minutes. Garnish with pimiento strips, if desired. Yield: 4 to 6 servings.

Note: 2 (10-ounce) packages frozen asparagus spears, thawed, may be substituted for fresh.

Front: Lemon-Roasted Chicken and New Potatoes. Left: Cheese Biscuits. Right: Tomato Aspic. Rear: Fresh Asparagus. With such a dinner, plus a Raspberry Fool, the Vernal Equinox is ushered in with style.

From a nineteenth-century advertising card.

RASPBERRY FOOL

1 quart fresh raspberries, washed
1 cup sugar
2 cups whipping cream
Vanilla cookies (optional)

Combine raspberries and sugar in medium saucepan. Let stand 10 minutes to extract juice. Cook over medium heat 10 minutes or until soft. Strain raspberries, discarding seeds. Chill thoroughly.

Beat whipping cream until soft peaks form; fold into fruit mixture. Spoon into individual serving dishes; chill until firm. Serve with vanilla cookies, if desired. Yield: 4 to 6 servings.

Note: 2 (10-ounce) packages frozen raspberries, thawed and drained, may be substituted for fresh. Omit sugar in recipe.

Raspberry Fool with cookies.

NEW POTATOES WITH PARSLEY BUTTER

1¾ pounds new potatoes, washed and scrubbed
¼ cup butter or margarine, melted
⅓ cup chopped fresh parsley
Salt and pepper to taste

Pare a 1-inch strip around center of each potato, if desired. Cover potatoes with water; cook, covered, over medium heat 25 minutes or until tender. Drain, and set aside.

Combine remaining ingredients, stirring well. Pour over potatoes, coating thoroughly. Yield: 4 to 6 servings.

CHEESE BISCUITS

1 cup all-purpose flour
1½ teaspoons baking powder
¼ teaspoon salt
¼ cup shortening
½ cup (2 ounces) shredded sharp Cheddar cheese
⅓ cup milk

Combine flour, baking powder, and salt; cut in shortening and cheese until mixture resembles coarse meal. Add milk, stirring until moistened. Turn dough out onto a lightly floured surface, and knead lightly 3 or 4 times.

Roll dough to 1-inch thickness; cut into rounds with a 2-inch cutter. Place biscuits on a lightly greased baking sheet; bake at 450° for 10 to 12 minutes. Yield: about 1½ dozen.

SPRINGTIME SUNDAY DINNER

At the turn of the century, a foods writer in New Orleans stated that in that city only three vegetables ever had to be purchased in cans: asparagus, truffles, and mushrooms. Otherwise, with the annual multiple cropping carried on in the lower South, garden vegetables lasted just about all year long. Supermarkets aside, most of us look forward to that first pale ruffle of lettuce peeking above the soil and the unmistakable green shoots of the onion sets we put out earlier. Somehow, we traditionally think of ham at Easter, so here it is with raisin sauce to complement it.

BAKED HAM WITH RAISIN SAUCE
GREEN BEANS WITH POTATOES
WILTED LETTUCE SALAD
SPRING ONIONS AND GARDEN RADISHES
POPOVERS
EASTER DAWN CAKE
or
FRESH STRAWBERRIES
WITH CREAM

Serves 6

BAKED HAM WITH RAISIN SAUCE

In this up-dated recipe, cola takes the place of the cider or water often called for in early recipes.

1 (6½- to 7-pound) uncooked ham
Whole cloves
1 quart cola-flavored carbonated beverage
2 to 3 teaspoons ground cloves
1 to 2 teaspoons pepper
Raisin Sauce

Score fat on ham in a diamond design; stud with whole cloves. Place ham, fat side up, on a rack in a shallow roasting pan. Pour cola over ham, and sprinkle with ground cloves and pepper.

Bake ham, uncovered, at 325° for 3 to 3½ hours, basting frequently. Remove ham from roaster, discarding pan drippings. Cool ham thoroughly; slice and serve with Raisin Sauce. Yield: 10 to 12 servings.

Late nineteenth-century butcher's receipt from V. Hechler, Jr., & Brothers, Richmond, Virginia.

Raisin Sauce:
¾ cup firmly packed brown sugar
¾ tablespoon all-purpose flour
¼ cup plus 2 tablespoons vinegar
2½ cups water
3 tablespoons prepared mustard
¾ cup raisins

Combine sugar and flour in a heavy saucepan; stir well. Add remaining ingredients; bring mixture to a boil. Reduce heat; simmer 30 minutes or until thickened. Yield: 4 cups.

GREEN BEANS WITH POTATOES

1½ pounds fresh green beans
1 quart water
4 slices bacon
2 pounds new potatoes,
 washed and scrubbed
1 teaspoon salt
¼ teaspoon pepper

Wash beans, trim ends, and remove strings; break into 2-inch lengths. Place water, bacon, and beans in a Dutch oven; bring to a boil. Reduce heat; cover, and simmer 10 minutes or until crisp-tender.

Add potatoes, salt, and pepper; stir gently. Cover and cook 20 minutes or until tender. Yield: 6 servings.

WILTED LETTUCE SALAD

½ pound bacon
1 head iceberg lettuce
1 head Boston lettuce
½ cup tarragon vinegar
¼ teaspoon pepper
⅛ teaspoon seasoned salt

Cook bacon until crisp; drain, reserving pan drippings. Crumble bacon, and set aside.

Tear lettuce into bite-size pieces in a salad bowl. Sprinkle with crumbled bacon. Add vinegar, pepper, and salt to drippings in pan; bring to a boil. Pour warm dressing over lettuce, and toss lightly to coat well. Serve immediately. Yield: 6 to 8 servings.

POPOVERS

1 cup all-purpose flour
½ teaspoon salt
2 eggs
1 cup milk

Sift together flour and salt; set aside.

Combine eggs and milk; beat until frothy. Add dry ingredients. Beat just until blended.

Place 8 well-greased 4-ounce custard cups on a baking sheet in oven at 425° for 3 minutes or until a drop of water sizzles in cups. Remove from oven; spoon batter into cups, filling each half full. Bake at 425° for 20 minutes; reduce heat to 300°, and bake an additional 20 minutes. Serve. Yield: 8 popovers.

Picking beans in the fields of a Virginia farm.

EASTER DAWN CAKE

⅔ cup butter or margarine,
  softened
1¾ cups sugar
2 eggs
3 cups sifted cake flour
2½ teaspoons baking powder
1 teaspoon salt
1¼ cups milk
1½ teaspoons vanilla extract
6 drops red food coloring
3 drops oil of peppermint
Easter Dawn Frosting

Cream butter; gradually add sugar, beating well. Add eggs, one at a time, beating well after each addition.

Combine flour, baking powder, and salt; add to creamed mixture alternately with milk, beginning and ending with flour mixture. Mix well after each addition. Stir in vanilla.

Pour two-thirds batter into 3 greased and floured 8-inch round cakepans.

Add food coloring and oil of peppermint to the remaining batter. Spoon pink batter equally into batter in 3 pans. Swirl pink batter into white batter to obtain a marbled effect.

Bake at 350° for 25 minutes or until a wooden pick inserted in center comes out clean. Cool in pans 10 minutes; remove layers from pans, and let cool completely.

Spread Easter Dawn Frosting between layers and on top and sides of cooled cake. Yield: one 3-layer cake.

Easter Dawn Frosting:

4 egg whites
4½ cups sifted powdered
  sugar
1 cup butter or margarine,
  softened
1 teaspoon vanilla extract
Dash of salt
10 drops red food coloring

Beat egg whites (at room temperature) at medium speed of electric mixer until frothy. Gradually add sugar, beating at high speed until stiff peaks form. Add remaining ingredients; beat until smooth. Yield: enough for one 3-layer cake.

The popover in this menu is a member of an old and interesting family of hollow breadstuffs. Complement your menu by sprinkling the custard cups with sugar, flour, or Parmesan cheese. With very small changes, popover batter poured into the fat generated by the roasting of beef becomes the ancestral English Yorkshire pudding. Another change, with butter and more flour to stiffen the mixture, and we have that delicious old friend, the cream puff. Or we can make the batter thinner, pour it into sizzling hot butter in a large skillet, and bake it. And presto! the German pancake, toothsome and amusing-looking, with huge bubbles baked in. Even pita bread, the enchanting "pocket bread" of the Middle East, is a cousin of the popover, although made with olive oil and water. It bakes up into a marvelous balloon and sometimes has to be subdued with damp towels before it settles down with its hidden pocket ready to be filled for the world's oldest form of sandwich.

SUMMER SHORELINE SPECTACULAR

olonists arriving on our Eastern seaboard found oysters and other sea delicacies so plentiful that they had formed shoals that made navigating hazardous. That danger is past, but from Maryland to Texas, the ocean affords the South one of the richest seafood harvests in the world.

Red snappers are all-important to our fishing industry. And baked, broiled, or fried, snapper is a treat even to those living near the source. Landlocked seafood lovers can usually rely on the "flown-in-fresh-daily" fish houses. It's best to be there when the fishmonger drives in with his "catch."

BAKED STUFFED RED SNAPPER
CORN OYSTERS
FRESH GREEN PEAS
ORANGE DRESSING * FRESH FRUIT SALAD
CHOCOLATE MERINGUE PIE

Serves 6 to 8

BAKED STUFFED RED SNAPPER

1 pound fresh shrimp, peeled and deveined
1 large onion, chopped
2 cloves garlic, minced
1 tablespoon shortening, melted
¼ cup water
6 slices bread
1 small green pepper, finely chopped
2 tablespoons chopped fresh parsley
1 tablespoon chopped celery
¾ pint fresh oysters, drained and chopped
¾ teaspoon salt
¼ teaspoon pepper
1 bay leaf
Dash of dried whole thyme
8 red snapper fillets (about 4 pounds)
Creole Sauce
Fresh parsley sprigs (optional)

Sauté shrimp, onion, and garlic in shortening in a large skillet about 15 minutes over medium heat.

Sprinkle water over bread; mash and add to shrimp mixture. Add next 8 ingredients; simmer 10 minutes.

Place 4 fillets on a large broiler pan; evenly spoon one-fourth of stuffing mixture on each fillet. Top with reserved fillets, and fasten with wooden picks. Pour Creole Sauce over stuffed fillets.

Bake at 350° for 30 minutes or until fillets flake easily when tested with a fork.

Transfer stuffed fillets to a large serving platter; garnish with fresh parsley sprigs, if desired. Yield: 8 servings.

Note: 1 (5- to 7-pound) red snapper may be substituted for the fillets.

Creole Sauce:

2 large onions, finely chopped
2 cloves garlic, minced
1 green pepper, finely chopped
2 tablespoons chopped fresh parsley
2 bay leaves
Dash of dried whole thyme
1 tablespoon shortening, melted
1 tablespoon all-purpose flour
1 (16-ounce) can tomatoes, undrained and chopped

Sauté first 6 ingredients in shortening in a large skillet about 15 minutes over low heat. Add flour, and cook 1 minute, stirring constantly. Stir in tomatoes; simmer 10 minutes. Yield: about 2½ cups.

CORN OYSTERS

1¾ cups all-purpose flour
1 tablespoon sugar
1 teaspoon baking powder
½ teaspoon salt
1 (17-ounce) can whole kernel corn, undrained
1 egg, beaten
2 tablespoons milk
1½ cups shortening

Combine flour, sugar, baking powder, and salt; mix well. Combine corn, egg, and milk; stir into dry ingredients.

Heat shortening in large skillet over medium heat to 375°; drop corn mixture by tablespoonfuls into skillet. Cook until golden, turning once. Drain on paper towels. Serve hot. Yield: about 2 dozen.

Corn Oysters (rear) and Baked Stuffed Red Snapper (front), one of the tastiest seagoing delights.

FRESH GREEN PEAS

4 pounds fresh green
 peas
¼ cup butter or margarine,
 softened
1 teaspoon lemon juice
1 teaspoon salt
½ teaspoon pepper

Shell and wash peas. Place in medium saucepan, and add boiling water to cover. Cover, and cook over medium heat 10 to 12 minutes or until peas are tender.

Add butter, lemon juice, salt, and pepper to peas, stirring well. Yield: 6 to 8 servings.

ORANGE DRESSING

⅓ cup orange juice
1½ tablespoons lemon juice
1 egg, beaten
1 cup sugar
1 cup whipping cream,
 whipped
Pinch of salt

Combine juice, egg, and sugar in top of double boiler. Place over boiling water; cook, stirring constantly, about 10 minutes. Cool completely; fold in whipped cream and salt. Chill thoroughly. Serve Orange Dressing over fresh fruit in season. Yield: about 2 cups.

Collection of Bonnie Slotnick

CHOCOLATE MERINGUE PIE

1¼ cups sugar
½ cup cocoa
⅓ cup cornstarch
¼ teaspoon salt
3 cups milk
3 eggs, separated
3 tablespoons butter or
 margarine
1½ teaspoons vanilla extract
1 baked 9-inch pastry shell
¼ teaspoon cream of tartar
6 tablespoons sugar

Combine first 4 ingredients in a heavy saucepan. Mix well to remove lumps. Gradually add milk, stirring until blended. Cook over medium heat, stirring constantly, until mixture thickens and comes to a boil; boil 1 minute, stirring constantly. Remove from heat.

Beat egg yolks until thick and lemon colored. Stir one-fourth of hot mixture into yolks; add to remaining hot mixture, stirring constantly. Cook over medium heat 2 minutes, stirring constantly. Remove from heat; stir in butter and vanilla. Pour into pastry shell.

Combine egg whites (at room temperature) and cream of tartar; beat until foamy. Gradually add remaining sugar, 1 tablespoon at a time, beating until stiff peaks form. Spread over filling, sealing to edge of pastry. Bake at 400° for 8 minutes or until lightly browned. Cool. Yield: one 9-inch pie.

COUNTRY-STYLE SUMMER FEAST

anglewood, the home of Mr. and Mrs. William Neal Reynolds, was a working farm on the Yadkin River, not far from Winston-Salem, North Carolina. Childless, they were "Aunt Kate and Uncle Will" to swarms of young relatives, who reveled in Uncle Will's tales of the old days in Patrick County and in Aunt Kate's bountiful meals. "Dinner and supper always included meat and several vegetables. . . and dessert twice a day, usually some kind of pie. . . ." This is the sort of dinner which Mrs. Reynolds might have served her young admirers who visited at Tanglewood.

SOUTHERN FRIED CHICKEN
BAKED STUFFED SQUASH
SUMMER SALAD
CUCUMBERS IN SOUR CREAM
DEVILED EGGS
COUNTRY BISCUITS
BERRY ROLY-POLY

Serves 8

SOUTHERN FRIED CHICKEN

2 (2½- to 3-pound) broiler-fryers, cut into 16 pieces
1 tablespoon plus 2 teaspoons salt
Pepper to taste
2½ cups all-purpose flour
3 to 4 cups vegetable oil
2 cups milk
Hot cooked rice

Sprinkle chicken with salt and pepper; dredge in flour. Set 3 tablespoons flour aside.

Heat oil to 375° in a 10-inch cast-iron skillet. Brown 4 chicken pieces for 12 to 15 minutes. Drain well on paper towels. Repeat procedure with remaining chicken.

Drain oil from skillet, reserving 3 tablespoons pan drippings in skillet. Add reserved flour to pan drippings, stirring until smooth. Cook 1 minute, stirring constantly. Gradually add milk to mixture in skillet; cook over medium heat, stirring constantly, until thickened and bubbly. Serve gravy with chicken and hot cooked rice. Yield: 8 servings.

BAKED STUFFED SQUASH

8 medium-size yellow squash
8 slices bacon, cooked and crumbled
½ cup finely chopped pecans
1 tablespoon minced fresh parsley
⅓ cup butter or margarine
¼ cup half-and-half
1½ teaspoons onion juice
¼ teaspoon salt
¼ teaspoon pepper
About ⅔ cup cracker crumbs
Grated Parmesan cheese

Wash squash; cook in boiling salted water to cover 10 to 12 minutes or until tender but still firm. Drain, and cool slightly.

Trim off stems, and cut squash in half lengthwise. Remove and reserve pulp, leaving a firm shell.

Combine next 8 ingredients with squash pulp; stir well. Gradually add cracker crumbs until mixture holds together.

Place squash shells in an ungreased 13- x 9- x 2-inch baking dish. Spoon stuffing evenly into shells; sprinkle with Parmesan cheese. Bake at 350° for 25 minutes or until lightly browned. Yield: 8 servings.

SUMMER SALAD

4 medium tomatoes, peeled and sliced
2 medium-size green peppers, sliced into thin rings
1 small onion, chopped
2 tablespoons sugar
2 tablespoons vinegar
½ teaspoon salt
½ teaspoon pepper

Combine first 3 ingredients; toss gently, and set aside.

Combine remaining ingredients; stir well, and pour over vegetables. Toss gently; cover and chill 8 to 10 hours. Drain before serving. Yield: 8 servings.

CUCUMBERS IN SOUR CREAM

4 medium cucumbers
1½ teaspoons salt
6 radishes, minced
1 (8-ounce) carton commercial sour cream
1 tablespoon plus 1 teaspoon minced onion
1 teaspoon lemon juice
¼ teaspoon salt
¼ teaspoon pepper
Sliced radishes (optional)

Slice cucumbers into a medium bowl; sprinkle with 1½ teaspoons salt, and chill 1 hour. Drain on paper towels, pressing to remove liquid. Return to bowl; stir in remaining ingredients, tossing gently. Chill. Garnish with sliced radishes, if desired. Yield: 8 servings.

DEVILED EGGS

1 dozen hard-cooked eggs
½ cup mayonnaise
1 tablespoon minced onion
2 teaspoons prepared
  mustard
¼ teaspoon salt
Dash of pepper
Paprika
12 slices pimiento-stuffed
  olives
Shredded lettuce

Cut eggs in half lengthwise; remove yolks. Mash yolks; stir in next 5 ingredients.

Generously spoon yolk mixture over cut side of 12 egg white halves. Top with remaining egg white halves, cut side down; press gently. Sprinkle with paprika, and garnish with olive slices. Serve on shredded lettuce. Yield: 8 to 12 servings.

Deviled Eggs, Summer Salad, Cucumbers in Sour Cream

COUNTRY BISCUITS

2 cups all-purpose flour
1 tablespoon baking powder
2 teaspoons sugar
½ teaspoon salt
½ teaspoon baking soda
½ teaspoon cream of tartar
½ cup shortening
¾ cup buttermilk

Sift dry ingredients. Cut in shortening until mixture resembles coarse meal. Add buttermilk to flour mixture, stirring until dry ingredients are moistened. Turn out onto a lightly floured surface; knead lightly 3 to 5 times or until smooth.

Pat dough out to ½-inch thickness; cut with a 2¼-inch biscuit cutter. Place biscuits on a lightly greased baking sheet. Bake at 450° for 10 minutes. Yield: 1½ dozen.

BERRY ROLY-POLY

3 cups all-purpose flour
2 tablespoons sugar
1 teaspoon salt
½ cup butter or margarine
½ cup shortening
¼ cup plus 2 tablespoons
  ice water
1 tablespoon butter or
  margarine, melted
1 quart fresh blackberries
1 pint fresh raspberries
1½ cups sugar
½ teaspoon ground nutmeg
½ cup whipping cream,
  whipped

Combine flour, 2 tablespoons sugar, and salt; cut in ½ cup butter and shortening with pastry blender until mixture resembles coarse meal. Sprinkle ice water evenly over surface, stirring until ingredients can form a ball.

Turn dough out onto a lightly floured cloth. Roll into a 16- x 12-inch rectangle. Brush 1 tablespoon melted butter over surface of pastry.

Combine blackberries, raspberries, 1½ cups sugar, and nutmeg, tossing lightly to coat well. Spread evenly over pastry.

Starting at long edge, roll up dough jellyroll fashion; press seam to seal. Cut berry roll in half; place each half on a lightly greased 10- x 6- x 2-inch baking dish. Bake at 400° for 20 minutes; reduce heat to 350°, and bake 50 to 55 minutes. Cool slightly, and cut into slices. Serve with a dollop of whipped cream. Yield: about 16 servings.

Note: 2 (10-ounce) packages frozen raspberries, thawed and drained, may be substituted for fresh. One roll may be frozen.

HARVEST TIME

Make yourself at home!" What a marvelous thing to hear upon entering the home of a friend . . . or to say when a friend enters yours. And especially in the fall, when gardens deliver their final outpouring of vegetables. No one will deny that digging sweet potatoes or picking greens is work. But the home vegetable grower will tell you the satisfaction he gets from seeing his effort rewarded and the pleasure he takes in sharing the wealth of his dinner table are well worth the toil. Now is the time to use those crispy fall apples, and dig into a pot of greens.

PORK LOIN ROAST
GLAZED FRIED APPLES
SWEET POTATO SOUFFLÉ
AUTUMN GREENS
CORNBREAD MUFFINS
PERSIMMON PUDDING

Serves 6 to 8

PORK LOIN ROAST

1 (4- to 5-pound) pork loin roast
1 teaspoon salt
½ teaspoon pepper
2 tablespoons all-purpose flour
2 medium onions, chopped
1 carrot, cut into ½-inch slices
1 stalk celery
7 to 8 large sprigs fresh parsley
½ teaspoon dried thyme leaves
1 bay leaf, crushed
4 cups water, divided
⅓ cup firmly packed brown sugar
2 tablespoons all-purpose flour
1 to 1½ cups water

Rub roast with salt and pepper; dust with 2 tablespoons flour. Place roast, fat side up, on rack in a roasting pan. Insert meat thermometer, making certain thermometer does not touch bone or fat. Place onion, carrot, celery, and parsley around meat. Sprinkle meat with thyme and bay leaf.

Pour 2 cups water in roasting pan; add remaining 2 cups water as needed for basting.

Roast pork at 350° for 2½ hours or until roast reaches 170°, basting often with juices in pan. Sprinkle brown sugar over roast during last 30 minutes of baking. Let stand 10 to 15 minutes.

Remove roast, parsley, carrot, and celery; reserve pan drippings. Combine 2 tablespoons flour and 1 to 1½ cups water; stir until smooth. Pour flour mixture into pan drippings; cook, stirring constantly, until thickened and bubbly. Serve gravy with roast. Yield: 6 to 8 servings.

GLAZED FRIED APPLES

4 medium apples, unpeeled and cored
¼ cup plus 2 tablespoons butter or margarine
¼ cup sugar
¼ cup firmly packed brown sugar

Slice apples into ⅛-inch rings. Place apples and butter in a large skillet; cover and cook over medium heat 10 minutes or until apples are tender. Add sugar, and cook uncovered 10 minutes or until golden brown. Yield: 6 to 8 servings.

SWEET POTATO SOUFFLÉ

3 cups cooked, mashed sweet potatoes
1 cup sugar
3 eggs
1 teaspoon vanilla extract
½ cup milk
¼ cup butter or margarine, softened
Dash of salt
1 cup firmly packed brown sugar
½ cup self-rising flour
¼ cup butter or margarine, softened
1 cup chopped pecans

Combine potatoes, sugar, eggs, vanilla, milk, ¼ cup butter, and salt; beat at medium speed of an electric mixer until smooth. Spoon into a greased, shallow 2-quart casserole. Combine brown sugar, flour, ¼ cup butter, and pecans; sprinkle over top of potato mixture. Bake at 350° for 35 to 40 minutes. Yield: 6 to 8 servings.

A harvest of good food: Glazed Fried Apples, Cornbread Muffins, Pork Loin Roast, Sweet Potato Soufflé, and Autumn Greens.

AUTUMN GREENS

4½ pounds turnip greens
¾ to 1 pound salt pork,
   washed and diced
1½ cups water
1 cup chopped onion
1 teaspoon sugar
½ teaspoon pepper

Cut off and discard tough stems and discolored leaves from greens. Wash greens thoroughly and drain.

Cook salt pork in a large Dutch oven over medium heat, stirring frequently, until crisp and brown.

Add greens, water, onion, sugar, and pepper; bring to a boil. Reduce heat, cover, and simmer 40 to 45 minutes or until greens are tender. Yield: 6 to 8 servings.

Many hands are needed to help with the fall harvest.

CORNBREAD MUFFINS

1 cup cornmeal
⅓ cup all-purpose flour
1 teaspoon baking powder
½ tablespoon sugar
¾ teaspoon salt
1 cup milk
1 egg
2 tablespoons bacon
   drippings

Combine first 5 ingredients; mix well. Add milk, egg, and bacon drippings; stir only to combine. Fill greased muffin pans two-thirds full. Bake at 450° for 15 minutes or until browned. Yield: 9 muffins.

PERSIMMON PUDDING

¼ cup butter or margarine,
   softened
½ cup sugar
½ cup firmly packed
   brown sugar
2 eggs
1½ cups all-purpose flour
¼ teaspoon salt
Pinch of baking soda
½ teaspoon ground cinnamon
½ cup milk
2 cups persimmon pulp
½ cup whipping cream
2 teaspoons brandy

Cream butter; gradually add sugar, beating well. Add eggs, one at a time, beating well after each addition.

Combine dry ingredients; add to creamed mixture alternately with milk, beginning and ending with flour mixture. Stir in persimmon pulp. Spoon into a greased, shallow 2-quart baking dish. Bake at 325° for 40 minutes or until set.

Combine whipping cream and brandy; beat until stiff peaks form. Serve over warm pudding. Yield: 6 to 8 servings.

NOVEMBER.

INDIAN-SUMMER DINNER

I ndian Summer. Time to drive the side roads and watch the foliage begin to color up, perhaps stop when a sign near a farmhouse says "Cider for Sale," or to picnic as often as possible, for we know this bonus of sunny days is nature's little trick to make us forget a cold snap is just around the bend. In the upper South, the nights grow nippy, and cords of firewood begin to grow in orderly piles against porch walls. It is a time of heightened awareness; the bees sound busier, and flowers seem the more beautiful. We will bake a cake with the cider and drink the rest.

ROAST BEEF WITH GRAVY
CREAMY POTATO CASSEROLE
GLAZED FRESH BEETS
MIXED GREENS WITH FRENCH DRESSING
HARVEST ROLLS
OCTOBER CIDER CAKE

Serves 6

ROAST BEEF WITH GRAVY

⅓ cup all-purpose flour
½ teaspoon salt
1 teaspoon pepper
1 (6- to 6½-pound) shoulder or chuck roast
2 tablespoons vegetable oil
5 cups water
2 tablespoons all-purpose flour
2 tablespoons water

Combine first 3 ingredients; dredge roast in flour mixture. Brown roast in hot oil in a large Dutch oven. Pour 5 cups water over roast. Bake at 325° for 3 hours or until tender. Baste roast with pan drippings at 30 minute intervals.

Remove roast to serving platter. Combine 2 tablespoons flour and 2 tablespoons water; stir into pan drippings. Cook over medium-high heat, stirring constantly, until thickened and bubbly. Serve gravy with roast. Yield: 10 to 12 servings.

CREAMY POTATO CASSEROLE

4 medium potatoes, peeled and cubed
1 teaspoon salt
1 cup chopped onion
½ cup chopped pimiento
¼ cup butter or margarine
¼ cup all-purpose flour
2 cups milk
⅛ teaspoon pepper
⅛ teaspoon salt
2 cups (8 ounces) shredded process American cheese
½ cup cracker crumbs
2 teaspoons butter or margarine

Combine potatoes and 1 teaspoon salt in a medium saucepan; add water to cover. Cook over medium heat 15 to 20 minutes or until tender; drain.

Combine cooked potatoes, onion, and pimiento; stir gently. Spoon into a greased 1½-quart casserole.

Melt ¼ cup butter in a small heavy saucepan over low heat; add flour, stirring until smooth. Cook 1 minute, stirring constantly. Gradually add milk; cook over medium heat, stirring constantly, until thickened and bubbly. Stir in pepper, ⅛ teaspoon salt, and cheese; cook, stirring constantly, until cheese is melted.

Pour cheese sauce over potatoes; sprinkle with cracker crumbs, and dot with 2 teaspoons butter. Bake at 350° for 30 minutes or until lightly browned. Yield: 6 servings.

Collection of Bonnie Slotnick

57

Harvest Hands at Dinner *by Clara Irene McDonald Williamson.*

GLAZED FRESH BEETS

24 medium-size fresh
  beets
1 cup sugar
1½ teaspoons cornstarch
½ cup water
½ cup vinegar
¼ cup butter or
  margarine

Trim beets leaving root and 1 inch of stem; scrub well with vegetable brush. Place beets in a saucepan, and add water to cover. Bring to a boil; cover and cook 35 to 40 minutes or until beets are tender. Drain. Pour cold water over beets; drain. Let cool. Trim off stems and roots, and rub off skins. Cut beets into ¼-inch slices. Set aside.

Combine sugar and cornstarch in a heavy saucepan; stir in water and vinegar. Cook over medium heat, stirring constantly, until thickened and bubbly.

Add beets to sauce, and cook 15 minutes; stir in butter. Yield: 6 to 8 servings.

FRENCH DRESSING

1¼ cups vegetable oil
1 teaspoon sugar
½ cup lemon juice
3 tablespoons chili sauce
1 teaspoon prepared
  horseradish
1 teaspoon prepared
  mustard
1 clove garlic, minced
1½ teaspoons salt
½ teaspoon paprika
¼ teaspoon pepper

Combine oil, sugar, and lemon juice; beat with wire whisk until blended. Add remaining ingredients; mix well. Store dressing in refrigerator. Yield: 2 cups.

HARVEST ROLLS

1 package dry yeast
¼ cup warm water (105°
  to 115°)
2½ cups milk
½ cup shortening
2 teaspoons sugar
5 cups all-purpose flour
1 teaspoon salt

Dissolve yeast in warm water, and set aside.

Scald milk; add shortening and sugar, stirring until shortening melts. Cool slightly. Add flour and salt; beat until smooth. Add yeast mixture; beat well.

Shape dough into a ball; place in a greased bowl, turning to grease top. Cover, and let rise in a warm place (85°), free from drafts, 1½ hours or until doubled in bulk.

Punch dough down. Fill well-greased muffin pans about one-third full. Cover, and let rise in a warm place 45 minutes or until doubled in bulk. Bake at 425° for 15 minutes or until golden brown. Yield: about 3 dozen.

OCTOBER CIDER CAKE

¾ cup shortening
1½ cups firmly packed brown
  sugar
3 eggs
3 cups all-purpose flour
1 tablespoon baking powder
¾ teaspoon salt
1 teaspoon ground nutmeg
1 teaspoon ground cinnamon
¼ teaspoon ground cloves
1 cup apple cider
1 tablespoon lemon juice
Cider Filling
Creamy Cider Frosting
Chopped pecans (optional)

Cream shortening; gradually add sugar, beating well. Add eggs, one at a time, beating well after each addition.

Combine flour, baking powder, salt, nutmeg, cinnamon, and cloves; add to creamed mixture alternately with cider, beginning and ending with flour mixture. Stir in lemon juice.

Pour batter into 3 greased and floured 8-inch round cakepans. Bake at 350° for 25 minutes or until a wooden pick inserted in center comes out clean. Cool in pans 10 minutes; remove layers from pans, and cool completely.

Spread Cider Filling between layers; spread top and sides with Creamy Cider Frosting. Garnish top of cake with pecans, if desired. Yield: one 3-layer cake.

Cider Filling:

½ cup sugar
3 tablespoons cornstarch
¼ teaspoon salt
1 cup apple cider
2 tablespoons lemon juice
2 tablespoons butter or
  margarine

Combine sugar, cornstarch, and salt in a heavy saucepan; gradually stir in cider. Cook over medium heat, stirring constantly, until thickened.

Remove from heat. Stir in lemon juice and butter; cool. Yield: about 1¼ cups.

Creamy Cider Frosting:

½ cup butter or margarine
¼ cup plus 1 tablespoon
  apple cider
¼ teaspoon salt
About 4½ cups sifted
  powdered sugar
½ cup chopped pecans

Combine first 3 ingredients in a heavy saucepan. Boil 1 minute, stirring constantly. Remove from heat; cool. Gradually add sugar until spreading consistency; beat until smooth. Add pecans. Yield: enough for one (8-inch) 3-layer cake.

October Cider Cake: Opulent eating for cider lovers.

*An early cider press
separating out
the apple juice.*

WINTER REPAST

T here is one good thing to be said for the cold months: they have Rs in them and bring us oysters in their season. We may also feel grateful for handed-down recipes such as Charleston Oyster Soup with just a trace of mace. If you were taking this meal with a South Carolina sportsman, the duck would probably be wood duck, the only migratory waterfowl that nests in the state. And the hunter would regale you with the happy misery of sitting quietly in the blind, waiting to call down that duck. Just listen and eat; he's proud of his heritage of living off the land.

CHARLESTON OYSTER SOUP
DUCKLINGS WITH APPLES AND RAISINS
BROWN RICE
PIQUANT BRUSSELS SPROUTS
SIXTY-MINUTE ROLLS
PUMPKIN-ALMOND CHARLOTTE

Serves 8

CHARLESTON OYSTER SOUP

1 tablespoon butter or margarine
1 quart oysters, undrained
1 cup water
1 tablespoon all-purpose flour
½ teaspoon salt
½ teaspoon pepper
⅛ to ¼ teaspoon ground mace
2 cups whipping cream
¼ to ⅓ cup sherry (optional)

Melt butter in a Dutch oven; add undrained oysters. Cook over medium heat, stirring constantly, until hot. Add next 5 ingredients. Gradually add cream, stirring constantly. Continue cooking over medium heat, stirring constantly, until mixture is heated and oyster edges curl. Stir in sherry, if desired. Yield: 6½ cups.

DUCKLINGS WITH APPLES AND RAISINS

2 (4- to 4½-pound) dressed ducklings
1 teaspoon salt
½ teaspoon pepper
3 stalks celery, chopped
3 apples, cored and chopped
¾ cup raisins
1 cup lemon juice
1 cup butter or margarine, melted
1 medium onion, chopped
1 stalk celery, chopped
1½ cups water
2 tablespoons all-purpose flour

Remove giblets from cavities of ducklings; set aside.
Rub cavities with salt and pepper. Combine 3 stalks chopped celery, apple, and raisins; spoon into cavity of each duckling. Close the cavity of duckling with skewers.
Combine lemon juice and butter; set aside.
Place ducklings, breast side up, on a rack in roasting pan. Bake, uncovered, at 350° for 1½ hours or until drumsticks and thighs move easily. Baste ducklings often with lemon-butter mixture during last 30 minutes of cooking time.

Combine onion, 1 stalk chopped celery, water, and giblets in a large saucepan; cover and cook over low heat until giblets are tender. Strain stock, and set aside. Discard vegetables. Chop giblets, and set aside.
Remove ducklings to serving platter. Degrease pan juices. Combine reserved stock and pan juices. Add flour; stir well. Add giblets; cook over medium heat until thickened. Serve gravy separately as a side dish. Yield: 8 to 10 servings.

BROWN RICE

7 cups water
2 cups uncooked brown rice
2 teaspoons salt
¼ cup butter or margarine, softened

Combine water, rice, and salt in a heavy saucepan; bring to a boil. Cover, reduce heat, and simmer 50 minutes or until all liquid is absorbed. Stir butter into rice. Yield: 8 servings.

Ducklings with Apples and Raisins on Brown Rice.

PIQUANT BRUSSELS SPROUTS

2½ pounds brussels sprouts
2 eggs
⅔ cup vinegar
⅓ cup water
¼ cup sugar
1 teaspoon salt
½ teaspoon dry mustard
¼ teaspoon pepper
12 slices bacon

Wash brussels sprouts thoroughly; drop into a small amount of boiling salted water. Return to a boil; cover, and cook 8 to 10 minutes or until tender. Drain; transfer to serving dish, and keep warm.

Beat eggs with electric mixer until thick and lemon colored; add next 6 ingredients, and mix well.

Fry bacon until crisp; drain, reserving ¼ cup pan drippings. Crumble bacon, and set aside. Add egg mixture to drippings in pan. Cook over low heat, stirring constantly, until thickened and bubbly. Pour dressing over brussels sprouts, and sprinkle with crumbled bacon. Serve immediately. Yield: 8 servings.

SIXTY-MINUTE ROLLS

1 package dry yeast
1½ cups warm milk (105°
  to 115°)
2 tablespoons shortening
2 tablespoons sugar
1 egg, slightly beaten
1 teaspoon salt
4 cups all-purpose flour

Dissolve yeast in warm milk. Add shortening, sugar, and egg; stir until shortening is melted. Stir in salt and flour to make a soft dough.

Place dough in a well-greased bowl, turning to grease top. Cover, and let rise in a warm place (85°), free from drafts, 15

Cooper River at Charleston, 1800s. Aquatint by W.J. Bennett.

minutes. Punch dough down; cover, and let rise in a warm place (85°), free from drafts, 15 minutes or until doubled in bulk.

Lightly grease muffin pans. Shape dough into 2-inch balls; place one in each muffin cup. Cover, and let rise in a warm place (85°), free from drafts, 15 minutes or until doubled in bulk. Bake at 400° for 15 minutes or until brown. Yield: about 2 dozen.

PUMPKIN-ALMOND CHARLOTTE

¼ cup light corn syrup
3 tablespoons dark rum
12 ladyfingers, split in half lengthwise
⅔ cup fine gingersnap cookie crumbs
2 envelopes unflavored gelatin
⅔ cup milk
⅓ cup dark rum
4 eggs, separated
⅓ cup firmly packed brown sugar
1 (16-ounce) can pumpkin
2 teaspoons grated orange rind
½ teaspoon pumpkin pie spice

⅓ cup firmly packed brown sugar
1 cup whipping cream, whipped
½ cup chopped almonds, toasted
Rum Cream
Sugar Almonds

Combine syrup and 3 tablespoons rum in a small bowl. Brush ladyfingers with syrup mixture, and dip into crumbs, coating both sides. Line sides and bottom of a 9-inch ungreased springform pan with prepared ladyfingers; set aside.

Combine gelatin, milk, rum, egg yolks, and ⅓ cup brown sugar in a medium saucepan; cook over low heat, 5 to 10 minutes, until thickened. Remove from heat, add pumpkin, orange rind, and pumpkin pie spice; stir well. Add ⅓ cup brown sugar; beat well.

Beat egg whites (at room temperature) in a large bowl, until stiff peaks form. Gently fold pumpkin mixture and whipped cream into egg whites. Fold in almonds. Pour mixture into prepared pan.

Cover, and chill at least 6 hours or overnight. Pipe rosettes of Rum Cream on top of charlotte, and sprinkle with Sugar Almonds to garnish. Yield: 8 to 10 servings.

Rum Cream:

½ cup whipping cream
2 tablespoons sifted powdered sugar
1 tablespoon dark rum

Beat cream until soft peaks form. Add sugar and rum; beat until stiff peaks form. Yield: about 1 cup.

Sugar Almonds:

½ cup slivered almonds
2 tablespoons sugar
½ teaspoon pumpkin pie spice

Combine all ingredients in a small saucepan; cook over medium heat, stirring frequently, until sugar is dissolved and almonds are well coated. Cool. Yield: about ½ cup.

COLD WEATHER SPECIAL, TEXAS-STYLE

A Texan can and will tell you all you need to know about chili. First, the meat should be either cubed or, next best, very coarsely ground. Second, chili contains no beans, spaghetti, or other adulterants. Red beans are, however, a respectable side dish. Nothing warms the bones so well in winter as a bowl of double hot chili: hot with heat and hot with chiles. While a salad is not mandatory, the contrast of something cool can be very comforting. Combine tart grapefruit with buttery avocado, found growing wild in Mexico by Cortez in 1519.

HOME-STYLE CHILI
TEXAS RED BEANS
GRAPEFRUIT-AVOCADO SALAD
FLOUR TORTILLAS
SOPAIPILLAS

Serves 8

HOME-STYLE CHILI

4½ pounds boneless round steak, finely diced
2 tablespoons vegetable oil
3 (14½-ounce) cans whole tomatoes, undrained
4 (4-ounce) cans chopped green chiles, undrained
2 cups water
1 teaspoon salt
¾ teaspoon ground cumin
¼ teaspoon red pepper

Brown steak in oil in a large Dutch oven. Add remaining ingredients; bring to a boil. Reduce heat, and simmer 2 to 3 hours, stirring frequently. Yield: 8 servings.
Note: If a thicker chili is desired, simmer an additional hour, stirring frequently.

TEXAS RED BEANS

2 pounds dried pinto beans
4 quarts water
1 pound salt pork, washed and diced
1 onion, chopped
1 clove garlic, minced
½ teaspoon salt

Sort and wash beans. Place in a large Dutch oven, and cover with water. Let soak overnight.

Add remaining ingredients, and bring to a boil. Reduce heat; cover and simmer 3 hours or until desired degree of doneness, adding water if necessary. Yield: 8 to 10 servings.

GRAPEFRUIT-AVOCADO SALAD

4 medium-size ripe avocados, peeled and sliced
2 tablespoons lemon or lime juice
4 medium-size pink grapefruits, peeled and sectioned
Leaf lettuce
Green or red maraschino cherries (optional)
French Dressing

Sprinkle avocado slices with lemon juice; toss well. Arrange avocado and grapefruit slices on lettuce leaves. Cover and chill 2 to 3 hours. Serve with French Dressing. Garnish with green or red maraschino cherries, if desired. Yield: 6 to 8 servings.

French Dressing:

1 cup olive oil
¼ cup vinegar
¼ cup lemon juice
2 teaspoons salt
1 teaspoon pepper

Combine all ingredients, mixing well; cover and refrigerate 1 to 2 hours. Yield: about 2 cups.

FLOUR TORTILLAS

4 cups all-purpose flour
2 teaspoons salt
⅛ teaspoon baking powder
⅔ cup shortening
1 cup plus 3 tablespoons hot water

Combine flour, salt, and baking powder; stir well. Cut in shortening with a pastry blender until mixture resembles coarse meal. Gradually stir in water, mixing well.
Shape dough into 1½-inch balls; roll each on a floured surface into a 6-inch circle.
Cook tortillas in an ungreased skillet over medium-high heat about 2 minutes on each side or until lightly browned. Pat tortillas lightly with spatula while browning the second side if they puff during cooking. Serve hot. Yield: about 2 dozen.

Bowls of Home-Style Chili (front) served with Texas Red Beans (rear) and Flour Tortillas (left center).

San Antonio's Military Plaza, *by Thomas Allen, c.1879.*

SOPAIPILLAS

1 package dry yeast
¼ cup warm water (105°
  to 115°)
4 cups all-purpose flour
1½ teaspoons salt
1 teaspoon baking
  powder
2 tablespoons sugar
1 tablespoon shortening
1½ cups milk, scalded and
  cooled
Vegetable oil
Powdered sugar
  (optional)
Honey (optional)

Dissolve yeast in warm water; let stand 5 minutes.

Combine flour, salt, baking powder, and sugar; cut in shortening. Make a well in center of mixture. Add yeast mixture and milk, mixing well. (Dough will be sticky).

Turn dough out onto a lightly floured surface, and knead 15 to 20 times. Roll dough to ¼-inch thickness; cut into 3-inch squares.

Heat ½ inch of oil in a large skillet to about 370°. Gently place dough squares in oil, a few at a time, lightly pressing down with a spatula until dough starts to bubble and puff. Turn and cook on other side until barely golden in color; drain. Sprinkle with powdered sugar or serve with honey, if desired. Yield: about 3 dozen.

Note: When frying sopaipillas, leave a few in skillet while adding additional ones. The ones left in the skillet will absorb the heat of the oil and keep it from overheating.

SOCIAL PASTIMES

Morning to Evening Entertainments

E ntertaining in the South, even among the most prominent folk, has become so casual that social events in our past read like those of another civilization. Yesterday's strictures and penchant for pomp, by today's standards, bordered on the ludicrous.

The New Year's Day open house or "at home" originated in New York. President Washington gave an open house the first New Year after his 1789 inauguration. Such a rage for this new form developed that, in order to keep from crossing paths on their way to one another's "at homes," people advertised the times of their parties in newspapers. Thus was born the party crasher, who, without knowing a soul, would make the rounds, toddling right in off the street. Public announcements ceased; the "at home" survived.

The South still observes customs that go back to grandmother's day: coming-out parties, bridal galas, even high teas. But the formality of "morning call" has given way to "coffee," and one sees less of the finger bowl, mint leaf afloat.

Parties may still be devilishly expensive, but the stiffness has gone out of them. At the presidential level, contrast the informal barbecues given for foreign dignitaries at the LBJ Ranch on the Pedernales with, say, later-to-be President Washington's 1784 Mt. Vernon reception for General Lafayette, who came to visit his old friend after the Revolutionary War.

By 1925, books on etiquette arrived to explain "style" to "new money." But books do not cover the ingrained habits of "old money." A Galveston girl was excised from her aunt's will in the 1920s for leaving the Thanksgiving table before the demitasse was served. The offended aunt was Mathilda Brown Sweeney, who had inherited Ashton Villa, the Italian Renaissance mansion built in Galveston by her father, James Moreau Brown, around 1860. The Brown family's holiday dinners lasted from two until seven, and that was that.

If the Creoles seem to outsiders to be born knowing how to have fun, put it down to early training. They may have grown up on weekly "soirées" given for them by their parents, with music, dancing, and simple refreshments. The "sirops" they served, and other endangered species, will be up-dated and remembered in this chapter.

MENU OF MENUS

NEW ORLEANS MORNING CUP

MORNING CALL

FOR LADIES ONLY LUNCHEON

TEAROOM LUNCHEON

BRIDGE PARTY AT ASHTON VILLA

AT HOME

COME FOR TEA

LAFAYETTE GINGERBREAD

CREOLE SOIRÉE

NEW ORLEANS MORNING CUP

"Belle calas tout chaud," came the cry of women peddling their hot rice cakes in the streets of old New Orleans. Nothing more delicious exists than those cakes, eaten with either café noir (black) or café au lait (with milk). Beignets, the French hollow doughnut-like day starter, may be easier to find; they, too, are soul-satisfying with coffee. New Orleans coffee, to the first-time visitor, usually comes as a shock. The traditional cup starts with a blend of rich, dark, strong coffee beans plus chicory. It sends you on your way, heart beating faster, panting for the next discovery. If you like a less hearty send-off, the Rich Café au Lait may be for you. The rich cream produces an even more delectable potion than the traditional "au lait."

CALAS
RICH CAFÉ AU LAIT
or
CAFÉ NOIR

Serves 6 to 8

CALAS

1½ cups hot cooked rice
½ package dry yeast
½ cup warm water (105°
  to 115°)
3 eggs, beaten
1¼ cups all-purpose flour
¼ cup sugar
½ teaspoon salt
¼ teaspoon ground nutmeg
Vegetable oil
Sifted powdered sugar

Mash rice grains, and cool to lukewarm. Dissolve yeast in warm water, and stir into rice. Cover, and let rise overnight in a warm place (85°), free from drafts.

Add eggs, flour, sugar, salt, and nutmeg to rice mixture, beating until smooth. Cover, and let stand in a warm place (85°) for 30 minutes.

Heat 3 inches of oil to 360°; drop dough by tablespoonfuls into hot oil. Cook about 3 minutes or until golden brown. Drain; sprinkle with powdered sugar. Serve immediately. Yield: 2½ dozen.

To start the day New Orleans style: Hot calas and Rich Café au Lait.

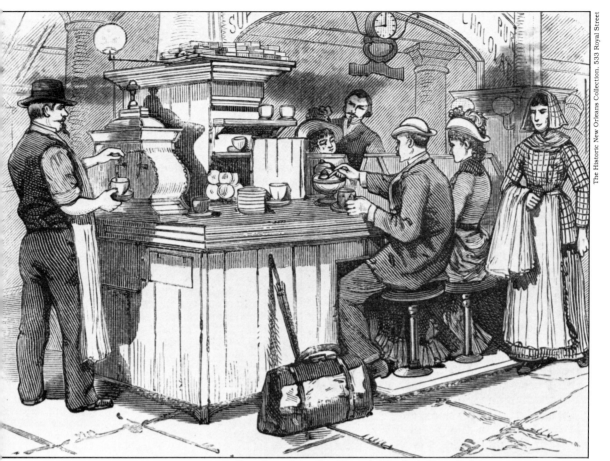

Coffee Stand in the French Market, New Orleans.

Label for coffee packaged in Louisiana, c.1900.

RICH CAFÉ AU LAIT

½ cup drip or finely ground
   mocha java coffee
4 cups boiling water
4 cups whipping cream
Sugar (optional)

Place coffee grounds in basket of a French drip coffee pot. Pour boiling water, a few tablespoonfuls at a time, over coffee grounds. Continue process until all water has dripped through grounds.

Bring cream to a boil.

To serve, pour ½ cup coffee and ½ cup cream in a serving cup. Add sugar, if desired, stirring well. Serve immediately. Yield: 8 cups.

Note: For Café Noir, omit whipping cream.

MORNING CALL

For several years before and after the Civil War, there flourished a social institution known as the "morning call." A house guest or out-of-town dignitary became an excuse to issue invitations to the social elite. The custom was that the guests roamed about looking at curios, art works, cut glass, and travel mementos, while enjoying confections and sandwiches served with tea and chocolate and coffee.

RIBBON SANDWICH LOAF
CHICKEN SANDWICHES
HEART AND DIAMOND SANDWICHES
MELTING DREAMS
MERINGUE BARS
STUFFED DATES
CHOCOLATE PEPPERMINT DAINTIES
CRYSTALLIZED ROSE PETALS AND MINT LEAVES
TROPICAL MINT PUNCH
HOT SPICED PUNCH
OLD-FASHIONED BOILED COFFEE

Serves 12 to 15

RIBBON SANDWICH LOAF

½ ripe avocado, mashed
1 tablespoon lemon juice
¼ teaspoon salt
2 (3-ounce) packages cream cheese, softened
¼ cup mayonnaise
2½ tablespoons finely chopped pimiento
1 teaspoon salt
1 large cucumber, peeled and thinly sliced
1 (3-ounce) package cream cheese, softened
2 (1-pound) loaves unsliced white bread
About ¼ cup butter or margarine, softened

Combine avocado, lemon juice, and ¼ teaspoon salt, mixing well. Chill.
Combine next 3 ingredients,

mixing well. Chill.
Sprinkle 1 teaspoon salt over cucumber slices; let stand 1 hour. Drain slices on paper towels, pressing to remove excess liquid. Finely chop cucumber; combine with remaining package of cream cheese, mixing well. Chill.
Trim crust from bread. Cut each loaf horizontally into four ½-inch-thick slices. Save remaining bread for other uses.
Spread softened butter on each slice of bread. Spread avocado mixture on bottom slice, pimiento mixture on second slice, and cucumber mixture on third slice. Stack slices, and cover with fourth slice. Wrap each loaf in waxed paper and a damp towel. Chill at least 5 hours. Slice each loaf in half lengthwise and in 12 slices crosswise. Yield: 4 dozen.

Stanton Hall in Natchez, Mississippi, completed in 1858, has been restored and is now open to the public.

CHICKEN SANDWICHES

1½ teaspoons salt
1½ teaspoons prepared mustard
2¼ teaspoons sugar
1 egg, beaten
2 tablespoons plus 1½ teaspoons butter or margarine, melted
¾ cup half-and-half
¼ cup vinegar
⅛ teaspoon onion juice
4 cups chopped cooked chicken
1 (16-ounce) loaf thinly sliced wheat bread
Pimiento slices
Pimiento-stuffed olives

Combine first 7 ingredients in top of double boiler; cook over boiling water for 15 minutes or until thickened. Remove from heat; cool. Add onion juice, stirring well. Stir in chicken.
Trim crust from bread, and cut into 2-inch rounds. Spoon chicken filling onto bread rounds. Decorate tops with pimiento slices and olives. Yield: about 4 dozen.

Combine flour, cornstarch, and sugar in a medium mixing bowl; cut in butter with pastry blender until mixture resembles coarse meal.

Shape dough into 1-inch balls, and place on ungreased baking sheets. Flatten balls with a fork in a crisscross pattern. Bake at 300° for 15 minutes or until lightly browned. Yield: 3 dozen.

MERINGUE BARS

½ cup butter or margarine, softened
¾ cup sugar, divided
3 eggs, separated
2 cups all-purpose flour
¼ teaspoon baking soda
¼ cup water
1 teaspoon vanilla extract
1 (16-ounce) jar orange marmalade
½ cup finely chopped pecans

Cream butter; gradually add ¼ cup sugar, beating until light and fluffy. Add egg yolks, one at a time, beating well after each addition.

Combine flour and soda; add to creamed mixture alternately with water, beginning and ending with flour mixture. Add vanilla; stir well.

Pat dough evenly in a greased 15- x 10- x 1-inch jellyroll pan. Spread orange marmalade evenly over dough in pan.

Beat egg whites (at room temperature) until frothy. Gradually add remaining sugar, 1 tablespoon at a time, beating until stiff peaks form. (Do not underbeat the mixture.) Spread meringue evenly over marmalade. Sprinkle pecans over top.

Bake at 350° for 25 minutes or until lightly browned. Cool. Cut into bars. Yield: 4½ dozen.

Crystallized confections, Melting Dreams, and Meringue Bars.

HEART AND DIAMOND SANDWICHES

1 (16-ounce) loaf thinly sliced white bread
About ¼ cup butter or margarine, softened
¾ cup cherry jam
1 (3-ounce) package cream cheese, softened
1 tablespoon plus 1 teaspoon half-and-half

Trim crust from bread. Cut a heart and a diamond shape from each slice of bread, using 2-inch diamond-shaped and 2½-inch heart-shaped cookie cutters. Spread each with butter and jam.

Combine cream cheese and half-and-half; mix well. Spoon cream cheese mixture into

pastry bag, and pipe around edge of each sandwich. Chill. Yield: 2½ dozen.

MELTING DREAMS

1¼ cups all-purpose flour
¼ cup cornstarch
½ cup sifted powdered sugar
¾ cup plus 2 tablespoons butter or margarine

STUFFED DATES

1 (8-ounce) package
  pitted dates
4 pecan halves
4 walnut halves
4 almonds
2 teaspoons peanut
  butter
4 candied cherries
1 large marshmallow,
  quartered
2 teaspoons candied
  orange peel
¼ cup sugar

Make a lengthwise slit in
dates. Stuff with a variety of the
next 7 ingredients; roll in sugar.
Yield: about 28 stuffed dates.

CHOCOLATE PEPPERMINT DAINTIES

½ cup butter, softened
1 (16-ounce) package
  powdered sugar, sifted
2 tablespoons milk
1 teaspoon vanilla extract
3 drops peppermint oil
¼ teaspoon salt
4 (1-ounce) squares
  unsweetened chocolate
1 tablespoon melted paraffin
  (optional)

Cream butter; gradually add
sugar, beating well. Stir in milk,
vanilla, peppermint oil, and
salt. Chill mixture overnight or
until firm. Shape into ¾-inch
balls.

Place paraffin, if desired, in
top of double boiler over boiling
water. Add chocolate, stirring
until melted. Using 2 forks,
quickly dip balls one at a time
into melted chocolate mixture.
Place dipped candies on waxed
paper, and refrigerate until
chocolate is firm. Yield: about 5
dozen.

CRYSTALLIZED ROSE PETALS AND MINT LEAVES

1 egg white
About 24 red rose petals,
  washed and drained
About 24 large mint leaves,
  washed and drained
About ¾ cup sugar

Beat egg white (at room temperature) until foamy. Using a
small pastry brush, coat each
rose petal and mint leaf with
beaten egg white. Brush lightly
to remove any excess egg white.
Immediately dip in sugar, coating well. Place on cooling rack.
Repeat procedure with remaining petals and leaves. Refrigerate overnight to dry. Yield: 4
dozen.

Note: These are edible and
may be used as a garnish.

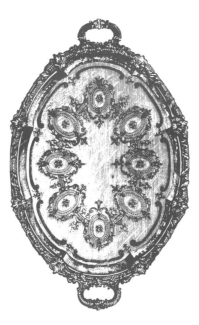

TROPICAL MINT PUNCH

1 quart strong hot tea
1½ cups sugar
1 cup mint leaves, washed
  and drained
1 quart pineapple juice
1 quart water
½ cup lemon juice
½ cup sifted powdered sugar
Ice ring

Combine first 3 ingredients.
Cover; let stand 15 minutes.
Strain tea; stir in pineapple
juice, water, lemon juice, and
powdered sugar. Cool. Serve in
a punch bowl over an ice ring.
Yield: about 12 cups.

HOT SPICED PUNCH

1 quart water
2 cups sugar
1 tablespoon grated lemon
  rind
½ cup lemon juice
2 (2-inch) cinnamon sticks
2 teaspoons whole cloves
1 quart grape juice
1 quart strong tea
Orange slices (optional)

Combine first 6 ingredients in
large Dutch oven; bring to a
boil. Reduce heat, and simmer
10 minutes; strain, and return
to Dutch oven. Stir in grape
juice and tea. Heat thoroughly;
serve hot with orange slices, if
desired. Yield: about 12 cups.

OLD-FASHIONED BOILED COFFEE

2 cups cold water, divided
1 cup regular grind coffee
4 egg shells, crushed
6 cups boiling water

Combine 1 cup cold water,
coffee, and egg shells in a large
saucepan. Add boiling water;
bring to a boil, and cook 4 minutes. Remove from heat; add remaining 1 cup cold water. Allow
to stand about 5 minutes.
Strain liquid; serve immediately. Yield: about 8 cups.

FOR LADIES ONLY LUNCHEON

When Bess Lindsay Gray of Winston-Salem announced her engagement in 1903, her friends outdid themselves in giving parties for her. "Of these, none could have been more elegant, more recherche . . . than the American Beauty luncheon tendered her . . . The red and green of the American Beauty idea prevailed in a

way throughout the nine courses of this delightful luncheon. . . ." Our up-dated bridal luncheon harks back to Miss Daisy's choice of foods: red and green grapes, cheese pudding, "Waldorf salad served in large red apples," and maraschino cream—a dessert that is the forerunner of what we know as Heavenly Hash.

CHEESE PUDDING
INDIVIDUAL APPLE SALADS
RED AND GREEN GRAPES
MARASCHINO CREAM

Serves 6

CHEESE PUDDING

10 slices bread
½ cup butter or margarine, melted
3 cups (12 ounces) shredded sharp Cheddar cheese
3 eggs
2 cups milk
½ teaspoon red pepper
½ teaspoon salt
½ teaspoon dry mustard
¼ teaspoon Worcestershire sauce
Fresh parsley sprigs (optional)

Remove crust from bread; cut bread into cubes, and toss with melted butter. Place half of bread cubes in a greased 2-quart baking dish. Sprinkle half of cheese over bread cubes. Repeat procedure with remaining bread cubes and cheese.

Combine remaining ingredients; beat well. Pour over top of casserole. Chill overnight.

Bake at 325° for 1 hour and 10 minutes or until lightly browned. Serve warm, and garnish with parsley sprigs, if desired. Yield: 6 to 8 servings.

Luncheon plates contain Cheese Pudding, Individual Apple Salads, and colorful red and green grapes.

A luncheon in elegant surroundings, Virginia, c.1920.

INDIVIDUAL APPLE SALADS

6 medium-size red apples
1½ cups chopped celery
½ cup seedless green grapes, chopped
½ cup chopped walnuts
½ cup mayonnaise

Cut a 1½-inch slice from top of each apple; reserve apple tops. Hollow each apple, leaving a ½-inch shell; chop pulp and set aside.

Combine pulp, celery, grapes, walnuts, and mayonnaise; mix well. Stuff each apple shell with about ⅓ cup apple mixture. Place apple tops over stuffed apples. Yield: 6 servings.

MARASCHINO CREAM

1 (15¼-ounce) can crushed pineapple, drained
1 (6-ounce) jar maraschino cherries, drained and chopped
1 cup chopped marshmallows
1 cup chopped pecans
½ teaspoon vanilla extract
1 cup whipping cream, whipped

Combine pineapple, cherries, marshmallows, pecans, and vanilla, stirring well. Fold in whipped cream.

Spoon into 6 sherbet glasses. Chill at least 4 hours. Yield: 6 servings.

LADIES' LUNCHEON

"It is an informal meal on ordinary occasions, when everything is placed upon the table at once. A servant remains in the room only long enough to serve the first round of dishes, then leaves, supposing that confidential conversation may be desired. Familiar friends often 'happen in' to lunch, and are always to be expected."

From Practical Cooking and Dinner Giving, 1877.

TEAROOM LUNCHEON

The tearoom was a phenomenon of the Depression. Two women who went into business with their kitchen skills were sisters, Willie Sterrett and Margaret Staten. Times were hard; they served bowls of chili on two card tables, later adding sandwiches and cookies. In 1931, they moved to Dallas' first shopping center, Highland Park Village, and in 1942, the S&S moved a few doors away, Mildred Liberton bought the tearoom in 1957 and it grew to sixty tables. Generations have grown up craving the good breads of the S&S, and the menu has changed little over the years.

CREAMED CHICKEN
SPINACH SOUFFLÉ
RASPBERRY-PINEAPPLE MOLD
BANANA NUT BREAD
DATE NUT BREAD
S&S CINNAMON ROLLS
STRAWBERRY MERINGUES

Serves 6

CREAMED CHICKEN

2 cups chopped cooked chicken
1 (4-ounce) can sliced mushrooms, drained
1 hard-cooked egg, chopped
½ medium-size green pepper, chopped
2 tablespoons chopped pimiento
3 tablespoons butter or margarine
¼ cup all-purpose flour
2 cups milk
1 cup chicken broth
1 teaspoon salt
½ teaspoon paprika
¼ teaspoon celery seeds
Toast points

Combine chicken, mushrooms, egg, green pepper, and pimiento. Set aside.

Melt butter in top of a double boiler over boiling water. Add flour, stirring constantly. Gradually add milk and chicken broth, blending well. Cook until thickened. Remove from heat; stir in salt, paprika, celery seeds, and chicken mixture, mixing well. Serve hot over toast points. Yield: 6 servings.

Note: May substitute chopped cooked shrimp for chicken.

SPINACH SOUFFLÉ

2 (10-ounce) packages frozen chopped spinach
1 tablespoon finely chopped onion
1 tablespoon butter or margarine
1½ tablespoons all-purpose flour
1 cup milk
¾ teaspoon salt
½ teaspoon pepper
4 eggs, separated
1½ cups (6 ounces) shredded sharp Cheddar cheese

Cook spinach according to package directions; drain and press dry. Set aside.

Sauté onion in butter in a heavy saucepan over low heat until tender. Blend in flour, stirring until smooth. Cook 1 minute, stirring constantly. Gradually stir in milk; cook over medium heat, stirring constantly, until thickened and bubbly. Stir in salt and pepper.

Beat egg yolks. Add one-fourth of hot white sauce to yolks, stirring well; return yolk mixture to white sauce. Add spinach and cheese; stir well.

Beat egg whites (at room temperature) until stiff but not dry.

Fold into spinach mixture. Spoon into a well-greased 2-quart casserole. Bake at 350° for 45 minutes or until golden brown. Yield: 6 to 8 servings.

RASPBERRY-PINEAPPLE MOLD

3 (3-ounce) packages raspberry-flavored gelatin
3¾ cups boiling water
1 (15¼-ounce) can crushed pineapple, undrained
2 (10-ounce) packages frozen raspberries, thawed and drained
3 bananas, diced
1 cup chopped pecans
Lettuce leaves (optional)
Mayonnaise (optional)

Dissolve gelatin in boiling water. Add pineapple to gelatin mixture, stirring well. Chill until mixture is consistency of unbeaten egg white.

Combine next 3 ingredients; fold into gelatin. Pour into a lightly oiled 9-cup ring mold; chill until firm. Unmold on lettuce leaves, and garnish with a dollop of mayonnaise, if desired. Yield: 6 to 8 servings.

BANANA NUT BREAD

¼ cup shortening
¾ cup sugar
1 egg
⅔ cup mashed ripe bananas
2 cups all-purpose flour,
   divided
½ teaspoon baking powder
½ teaspoon baking soda
¼ teaspoon salt
½ cup milk
1½ teaspoons vanilla extract
¾ cup chopped pecans

Cream shortening; gradually add sugar, beating well. Add egg; beat well. Add bananas, and mix until smooth.

Combine 1¾ cups flour, baking powder, soda, and salt; add to creamed mixture alternately with milk, beginning and ending with flour mixture. Stir in vanilla. Dredge pecans in remaining flour; stir into batter.

Pour batter into a greased and floured 9- x 5- x 3-inch loafpan. Bake at 350° for 1 hour. Cool in pan 10 minutes. Remove from pan, and cool completely on wire rack. Yield: 1 loaf.

DATE NUT BREAD

1 teaspoon baking soda
1 cup chopped dates
1 cup boiling water
1 tablespoon butter or
   margarine, softened
1 cup firmly packed dark
   brown sugar
1 egg
2 cups all-purpose flour,
   divided
½ teaspoon baking powder
¼ teaspoon salt
1 cup chopped pecans
1 teaspoon vanilla extract
1 (3-ounce) package cream
   cheese, softened (optional)

Sprinkle soda over dates; add water, and set aside.

Cream butter; gradually add sugar, beating well. Add date mixture and egg; beat well.

Combine 1¾ cups flour, baking powder, and salt; add to creamed mixture, beating until smooth. Dredge pecans in remaining flour; stir into batter. Stir in vanilla.

Spoon batter into a greased and waxed paper-lined 9- x 5- x 3-inch loafpan. Bake at 350° for 1 hour and 5 minutes or until a wooden pick inserted in center comes out clean. Cool in pan 10 minutes; remove from pan, and cool completely on wire rack. Slice, and serve with cream cheese, if desired. Yield: 1 loaf.

Tearoom favorites: S&S Cinnamon Rolls, sliced Banana Nut Bread, and Date Nut Bread loaf.

The newly-opened tearooms of the '20s and '30s were a perfect illustration of the connection between necessity and invention. Many a woman, finding her husband out of work, took steps to turn her kitchen skills into money, sometimes starting with only a room and two or three tables. As the proprietors were largely female, so was the clientele. Both sides benefited: Tearoom servings

S&S CINNAMON ROLLS

1 cup milk, divided
1 tablespoon shortening
¼ cup sugar
1½ teaspoons salt
2 packages dry yeast
½ cup warm water (105°
   to 115°)
About 4 cups all-purpose
   flour, divided
1 egg white
2 cups firmly packed brown
   sugar, divided
½ cup water
2½ tablespoons butter or
   margarine
1 cup flaked coconut
½ cup chopped pecans
1½ tablespoons ground
   cinnamon
2 cups sifted powdered sugar
2 tablespoons water

Scald ½ cup milk; add short-ening, ¼ cup sugar, and salt, stirring until sugar dissolves and shortening melts. Stir in re-maining ½ cup milk. Set aside.

Dissolve yeast in warm water; stir well. Let stand 5 minutes. Stir 2 cups flour into milk mixture, beating constantly. Add yeast mixture and ½ cup flour, stirring well.

Beat egg white (at room tem-perature) until stiff peaks form; fold into flour mixture. Stir in remaining flour (about 1½ cups) to make a soft dough.

Place dough in a greased bowl, turning to grease top. Cover, and let rise in a warm place (85°), free from drafts, 1 hour or until doubled in bulk. Divide dough in half; set aside.

Combine 1 cup brown sugar, ½ cup water, and butter in a saucepan; bring to a boil. Pour syrup into a lightly greased 15- x 10- x 1-inch jellyroll pan; set pan aside.

Turn half of dough out onto a lightly floured surface; roll into a 30- x 6-inch rectangle.

Combine remaining 1 cup brown sugar, coconut, pecans, and cinnamon; stir well, and sprinkle half of mixture evenly over dough. Roll up jellyroll fashion, starting at long side.

Pinch seams and ends together. Cut roll into 1-inch slices. Place slices, cut side down, in pre-pared jellyroll pan. Repeat pro-cedure with remaining dough and cinnamon mixture.

Cover, and let rise in a warm place (85°), free from drafts, 40 minutes or until doubled in bulk. Bake at 350° for 25 to 30 minutes. Combine powdered sugar and water, stirring well; drizzle over rolls. Serve warm. Yield: 4 dozen.

Note: Reheat frozen rolls at 250° for 10 minutes.

"Rosettes"
STRAWBERRIES WITH CREAM
DECORATED

STRAWBERRY MERINGUES

3 egg whites
¼ teaspoon cream of tartar
1 teaspoon vanilla extract
1 cup sugar
Vanilla ice cream
Sliced strawberries

Combine egg whites (at room temperature), cream of tartar, and vanilla; beat until frothy. Gradually add sugar, 1 table-spoon at a time, beating until stiff peaks form. (Do not under-beat the mixture.)

Spoon meringue into 6 equal portions on a well-greased bak-ing sheet. Using back of spoon, shape meringues into circles about 4 inches in diameter; shape each circle into a shell (sides should be about 1½ inches high). Bake at 275° for 55 minutes or until lightly browned. Turn off oven; leave meringues in oven for 1 hour for a crisper meringue. Cool away from drafts. Top with a scoop of ice cream and sliced strawber-ries. Yield: 6 servings.

were small and prettily served, appealing to the pre-sumed more delicate appe-tite of the feminine gender and an inexpensive way to lunch "out." One such entre-preneur was Alida Harper, who started a tearoom in her historic Pink House in Sa-vannah. In the 1936 photo-graph at left, she stands behind three of her wait-resses. Above is the interior of Hedrick's Restaurant called "Goodie Garden."

BRIDGE PARTY AT ASHTON VILLA

February 13, 1909. Dateline: Galveston. "Miss Alice Sweeney asked forty of her friends in for bridge whist yesterday afternoon at her home, Ashton Villa. Miss Sweeney, gowned in a crimson satin directoire robe, received her guests in the gold drawing room. The bridge tables were arranged in the living room and dining room. The guests who did not play cards remained in the drawing room and enjoyed a travelogue . . . this room is replete with treasures . . . and collections of Miss Rebecca Ashton Brown. . . ." The collation consisted of tarts, drop cakes, tea, and ices. Oh yes: The high scorer won a cut glass compote for her effort.

CHERRY ICE
VIENNA TARTS
DATE SQUARES
SPONGE DROP CAKES
TEA PUNCH

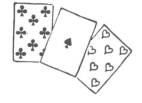

Serves 8

CHERRY ICE

2 cups sugar
¼ cup all-purpose flour
4 cups water
2 (16½-ounce) cans dark
    sweet cherries, undrained
½ cup lemon juice

Combine sugar, flour, and water in a large saucepan. Bring to a boil, stirring constantly until sugar dissolves; reduce heat, and simmer 3 minutes.

Drain cherries, reserving liquid. Add liquid and lemon juice to sugar mixture; stir well. Cool.

Place cherries in container of food processor or electric blender; process until smooth. Add to liquid mixture.

Pour mixture into freezer can of a 1-gallon hand-turned or electric freezer. Freeze according to manufacturer's instructions. Yield: 1 gallon.

For a dessert bridge party: Cherry Ice in stemmed glasses, surrounded by Vienna Tarts and Sponge Drop Cake with Date Squares in a compote. Tea Punch is the perfect beverage accompaniment.

Ashton Villa, built in 1860 by James Brown, hosted many grand-scale social gatherings.

VIENNA TARTS

1 (8-ounce) package cream cheese, softened
1 cup butter or margarine, softened
2 cups all-purpose flour
⅓ cup grape jelly

Combine cream cheese and butter in a medium mixing bowl; beat until smooth. Add flour, mixing well. Shape dough into a ball; chill for 30 minutes.

Roll pastry to ⅛-inch thickness on a lightly floured surface; cut dough into 2-inch squares. Place ¼ teaspoon of jelly in center of each square. Lift opposite corners of pastry squares, and pinch together in center. Repeat with remaining corners.

Place on an ungreased baking sheet; bake at 450° for 8 minutes or until lightly browned. Yield: about 2½ dozen.

DATE SQUARES

1 tablespoon butter or margarine, softened
1 cup sugar
2 eggs, beaten
1¼ cups sifted cake flour
1¼ teaspoons baking powder
½ teaspoon salt
1 tablespoon hot water
2 cups chopped dates
2 cups chopped pecans
Sifted powdered sugar

Cream butter; gradually add sugar, beating well. Add eggs; beat well.

Combine flour, baking powder, and salt; gradually add to creamed mixture, mixing well. Add water, and stir well. Add dates and pecans, stirring well (batter will be thick).

Spread batter in a greased 15- x 10- x 1-inch jellyroll pan. Bake at 300° for 35 to 40 minutes. Cool. Cut into 1-inch squares. Sprinkle with powdered sugar. Yield: about 9 dozen.

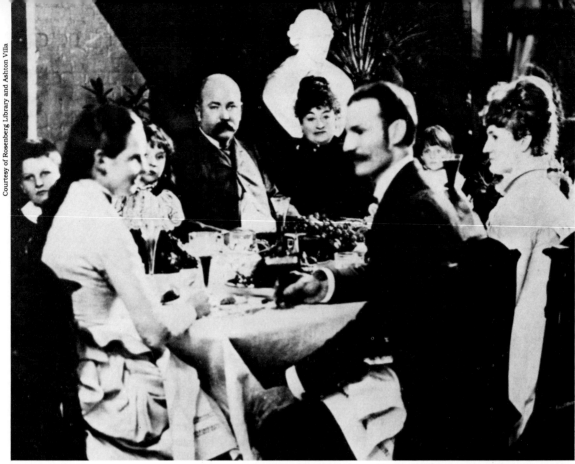

The Browns of Ashton Villa celebrate the holiday season of 1889 with a traditional family reunion dinner.

SPONGE DROP CAKES

3 eggs, separated
1 cup sugar
1 cup all-purpose flour
1 teaspoon baking powder
½ teaspoon vanilla extract
Chocolate Frosting
Grated chocolate
  (optional)

Beat egg yolks at high speed of an electric mixer until foamy. Gradually add sugar, beating until mixture is thick and lemon colored. Combine flour and baking powder; set aside.

Beat egg whites (at room temperature) until stiff peaks form; fold into yolk mixture. Fold flour mixture into batter, one tablespoon at a time. Fold in vanilla.

Spoon batter into well-greased miniature muffin pans, filling one-half full. Bake at 375° for 15 minutes. Remove from pans, and cool. Frost with Chocolate Frosting. Sprinkle with grated chocolate, if desired. Yield: 4 dozen.

Chocolate Frosting:

2 cups sifted powdered sugar
2 tablespoons butter or
  margarine, softened
3 tablespoons half-and-half
2 tablespoons cocoa

Combine all ingredients, beating until smooth. Yield: enough for 4 dozen miniature cupcakes.

TEA PUNCH

1 quart water
4 small tea bags
2 cups sugar
1 teaspoon ground cinnamon
1 teaspoon ground cloves
½ teaspoon ground nutmeg
1 (12-ounce) jar mint apple
  jelly
Grated rind of 1 orange
Juice of 4 oranges
Grated rind of 1 lemon
Juice of 3 lemons
2 cups grape juice
1 cup pineapple juice

Bring water to a boil in a large Dutch oven. Add tea bags; remove from heat, and cover. Let stand 10 minutes.

Remove tea bags, and add next 9 ingredients. Stir until jelly has dissolved.

Stir in grape and pineapple juices; cool. Serve over crushed ice. Yield: 2¾ quarts.

AT HOME

Social occasions and their evolution make for interesting reading. Our present-day "at homes" are outgrowths of the reception tea, or it could be argued that they are the same thing. We inherited the English tea as a daily rite, sometimes with only family present, sometimes a few friends. The hostess simply had a tray placed beside her favorite chair or in front of the sofa. Enlarged, tea was moved from the fireside to the dining room, and often the teapot was replaced by the punch bowl. In either case, the traditional cookies, cakes, and other "small foods" were served.

In the larger social centers of the South, such as Charleston or Atlanta, it became customary for would-be hostesses to announce in the local newspaper the times they would be "at home." However, this practice had to be abandoned when it became a common occurrence for complete strangers, having read the day's announcements, to wander in for free food and drink. Invitations for the informal "at home" may now be telephoned, although written ones are still in order if there is a guest of honor.

PEPPERY SPICED NUTS
CARAWAY CHEESE MOUND
SMOKED TURKEY ROLLS
SAUSAGE SWIRLS
PECAN SHORTBREADS
FILBERTS
MULLED CLARET

Serves 20 to 25

PEPPERY SPICED NUTS

4 cups pecan halves
2 tablespoons melted butter
2 teaspoons Worcestershire sauce
Dash of hot sauce
½ teaspoon salt
⅛ teaspoon pepper

Sauté pecan halves in butter in a skillet about 5 minutes. Add remaining ingredients, stirring well.

Place nut mixture in a shallow baking pan. Bake at 325° for 20 minutes, stirring occasionally. Yield: 4 cups.

CARAWAY CHEESE MOUND

2 cups butter, softened
4 (3-ounce) packages cream cheese, softened
2 tablespoons caraway seeds
2 teaspoons prepared mustard
2 teaspoons paprika

Combine butter and cream cheese, beating until smooth and creamy. Add remaining ingredients, blending well. Divide mixture in half, and mound each onto serving plate. Serve with assorted crackers. Yield: 2 cheese mounds.

SMOKED TURKEY ROLLS

24 thin slices smoked turkey
1 (8-ounce) package cream cheese, softened
Watercress
Paprika

Spread each slice of turkey with about 2 teaspoons cream cheese. Roll each slice lengthwise, jellyroll fashion. Cut each roll in half, and pierce with wooden pick to hold, if necessary. Tuck watercress into one end of each roll. Sprinkle with paprika. Yield: 4 dozen.

SAUSAGE SWIRLS

4 cups all-purpose flour
¼ cup cornmeal
2 tablespoons sugar
2 tablespoons baking
  powder
1 teaspoon salt
⅔ cup vegetable oil
¾ cup milk
2 pounds hot bulk pork
  sausage

Combine first 5 ingredients; blend in vegetable oil until mixture resembles coarse meal. Add milk, stirring until well blended. Turn dough out onto a lightly floured surface; knead lightly 3 or 4 times.

Roll dough into two 18- x 10-inch rectangles. Spread sausage (at room temperature) over dough, leaving a ½-inch margin on all sides. Carefully roll dough lengthwise, jellyroll fashion; pinch seam and ends to seal. Cover; chill at least 1 hour.

Slice dough into ¼-inch slices. Arrange 1 inch apart on baking sheets. Bake at 350° for 20 minutes or until lightly browned. Yield: 6 dozen.

Mulled Claret, Pecan Shortbreads, and filberts at Shirley Plantation.

PECAN SHORTBREADS

1 cup butter or margarine,
  softened
½ cup sifted powdered sugar
2¼ cups all-purpose flour
¼ teaspoon baking powder
½ cup finely chopped pecans

Cream butter; gradually add sugar, beating well. Combine flour and baking powder; gradually add to creamed mixture, mixing well. Stir in pecans. Cover, and chill 20 minutes or until dough is slightly firm.

Roll dough to ¼-inch thickness between sheets of waxed paper. Remove top sheet of waxed paper. Cut dough into desired shapes with a cookie cutter; remove excess dough. Place ungreased cookie sheet on top of cookies; invert and remove waxed paper.

Bake at 300° for 25 minutes or until lightly browned. Remove immediately to wire rack to cool. Yield: about 2½ dozen.

MULLED CLARET

4 (25.4-ounce) bottles dry red
  wine
2 cups firmly packed brown
  sugar
¼ cup lemon juice
4 (3-inch) cinnamon sticks
Lemon slices
Cinnamon sticks

Combine first 4 ingredients in a saucepan. Simmer 15 minutes. Pour in punch bowl with lemon slices. Serve with cinnamon sticks. Yield: 13 cups.

By the time President Washington gave his first New Year's "at home," or open house, party table settings were chiseled in stone and changed little until well into the nineteenth century. The tablecloth was white, "well washed and ironed . . . When taken from the table, it should be folded in the ironed creases, and some heavy article laid on it. A heavy bit of plank . . . " Pressed! or at least according to Miss Beecher in her "Domestic Receipt Book."

Taking a similar approach today, Helle and Hill Carter might offer drop-in guests at Shirley Plantation Mulled Claret served from a sterling silver punch bowl engraved with the head of Charles Carter's champion racehorse, Nestor. The James River can be seen through the window.

This 1870 engraving from Harper's Weekly *depicts a festive New Year's celebration.*

COME FOR TEA

Ladies of Athens, Georgia, enjoy tea on the porch, 1916.

"A woman never looks more attractive than when, becomingly gowned, she sits behind a dainty tea table, pouring the fragrant orange pekoe from a lovely old silver teapot into cups of eggshell thinness. It is thus you see the Englishwoman at her best. . . ." The foregoing is from a 1925 etiquette book, written by Anna Steese Richardson for Americans who yearned to do things the "right" way. One can envision Julia Gardiner Tyler in the 1800s serving tea in her Sherwood Forest home. The photograph (right) recreates such an occasion in the Sherwood Forest dining room where the present Mrs. Harrison Tyler might be found serving tea.

AMANDINE CHICKEN SANDWICHES
CUCUMBER-CHEESE SANDWICHES
TINY LEMON TARTS
FRESH FRUIT
TEA

Serves 12

AMANDINE CHICKEN SANDWICHES

⅓ cup mayonnaise
¼ teaspoon salt
¼ teaspoon curry powder
¼ teaspoon pepper
2 cups minced cooked chicken
½ cup blanched almonds, chopped
2 (16-ounce) loaves white bread
Pimiento strips (optional)

Combine first 4 ingredients, mixing well. Add chicken and almonds; mix well.

Remove crust from bread, and cut into rounds with a 2½-inch cookie cutter; slice each round in half, and spread with chicken mixture. Garnish with pimiento strips, if desired. Yield: about 3½ dozen.

CUCUMBER-CHEESE SANDWICHES

1½ cups small curd cottage cheese
½ cup seeded and diced cucumber
¼ cup fresh minced parsley
1 (16-ounce) loaf thinly sliced wheat bread
Cucumber slices

Combine first 3 ingredients, mixing well.

Remove crust from bread, and slice in half diagonally. Spread filling on each, and top with a cucumber slice. Yield: about 3 dozen.

Tiny Lemon Tarts are served in a tea setting with President Tyler's Rose Medallion China and his silver service, made by Mitchell & Tyler.

TINY LEMON TARTS

¾ cup sugar
1½ tablespoons cornstarch
1½ tablespoons all-purpose flour
Dash of salt
¾ cup water
2 eggs, slightly beaten
1 tablespoon butter or margarine
¼ teaspoon grated lemon rind
¼ cup lemon juice
12 baked 2-inch pastry shells
Whipped cream (optional)
Grated lemon rind (optional)

Combine sugar, cornstarch, flour, and salt in a medium saucepan. Gradually add water, stirring well. Cook over low heat, stirring constantly, until thickened and bubbly.

Gradually stir about one-fourth of hot mixture into eggs; add egg mixture to remaining hot mixture, stirring constantly. Cook 2 minutes over low heat, stirring constantly.

Remove from heat. Add butter, lemon rind, and juice; stir until butter melts. Cool slightly; spoon into pastry shells. Cool completely. Garnish with a dollop of whipped cream and grated lemon rind, if desired. Yield: twelve 2-inch tarts.

Lafayette visiting Washington at Mount Vernon in 1784, from the painting by Rossiter.

LAFAYETTE GINGERBREAD

George Washington and the Marquis de Lafayette began an enduring friendship during the Revolutionary War. In 1784, Lafayette visited his friend at Mount Vernon. Then, ". . . he went to Fredericksburg to pay his respects to the General's mother. They found her in her garden in short gown, petticoat and cap, raking leaves. Unaffectedly she greeted him, and together they went into the house where she made him a mint julep which she served with spiced gingerbread. . . ." Lafayette praised her son; she replied, "George was always a good boy."

MINT JULEP
LAFAYETTE GINGERBREAD

Mint Juleps should be made individually to serve any number of guests.

LAFAYETTE GINGERBREAD

½ cup butter
½ cup firmly packed brown sugar
1 cup molasses
3 eggs
3 cups all-purpose flour
1 teaspoon cream of tartar
2 tablespoons ground ginger
1 teaspoon ground cinnamon
1 teaspoon ground mace
1 teaspoon ground nutmeg
1 teaspoon baking soda
½ cup warm milk (105° to 115°)
½ cup brandy
2 tablespoons grated orange rind
⅓ cup orange juice
1 cup raisins

Plate, c.1825. "General Lafayette. Welcome to the land of liberty."

Cream butter; gradually add sugar, mixing well. Add molasses and eggs; beat well.

Combine flour, cream of tartar, and spices.

Dissolve soda in warm milk; add to creamed mixture alternately with flour mixture, beginning and ending with flour mixture; beat well after each addition. Stir in the remaining ingredients.

Pour batter into a greased and floured 13- x 9- x 2-inch baking pan. Bake at 350° for 35 minutes or until a wooden pick inserted in center comes out clean. Cool completely. Cut into squares to serve. Yield: 15 to 18 servings.

Mint Juleps and Lafayette Gingerbread: an historic snack.

MINT JULEP

1 teaspoon sifted powdered sugar
1 teaspoon water
3 to 5 fresh mint sprigs
3 ounces bourbon whiskey, divided
Fresh mint sprig

Combine first 3 ingredients in a serving glass; mull gently until sugar is dissolved. Add crushed ice, filling glass two-thirds full. Add 2 ounces bourbon; stir briskly. Add additional crushed ice to fill glass. Add remaining bourbon. Place glass in freezer; chill 15 minutes. Garnish with mint sprig. Yield: 1 serving.

CREOLE SOIRÉE

The "soirée" (evening entertainment) was very much a part of the young Creoles' growing up in old New Orleans and prepared them for the elaborate entertaining that was to become their way of life. The youngsters, with their fathers, would gather in the home of a friend to in-dulge their inherited fondness for music and dancing. The fathers would enjoy some strengthening libations, but these were not served to the young. Their refreshments were light and simple: the famous "sirops" served over crushed ice, petits fours, lemonade, and cooling ices.

WATERMELON ICE
SICILIAN ICE
POMEGRANATE ICE
PETITS FOURS
GRAPE AND BANANA SYRUPS
CHEESE WAFERS

Serves 10

WATERMELON ICE

1 small watermelon, peeled, seeded, and diced
1½ cups sugar
3 egg whites

Gradually add watermelon to container of electric blender, processing until smooth. Combine 10½ cups watermelon mixture and sugar in a large bowl; freeze until slushy. Beat well.

Beat egg whites (at room temperature) until stiff peaks form; fold into watermelon mixture.

Pour mixture into freezer can of a 1-gallon hand-turned or electric freezer. Freeze according to manufacturer's instructions. Yield: 2 quarts.

Note: Ice may be stored in freezer compartment of refrigerator until serving time. Let stand at room temperature 10 to 15 minutes before serving.

Watermelon Ice cools a summer evening. Serve with Petits Fours, a party food served at old-fashioned Creole soirées, and "Sirops," enjoyed by youngsters before the days of commercial soft drinks.

SICILIAN ICE

6 cups mashed peaches
1½ cups orange juice
2 cups sifted powdered sugar
½ cup whipping cream,
    whipped (optional)

Combine peaches, orange juice, and sugar; cook over medium heat until sugar is dissolved, stirring frequently.

Pour mixture into freezer can of a 1-gallon hand-turned or electric freezer. Freeze according to manufacturer's instructions. Serve with a dollop of whipped cream, if desired. Yield: about 2 quarts.

Note: 2 (16-ounce) packages of frozen sliced peaches, mashed, may be substituted for fresh peaches.

POMEGRANATE ICE

12 pomegranates
2 cups sugar
2 cups water

Peel pomegranates; carefully remove seeds, and press pulp through a food mill. Add sugar to pulp; stir until dissolved. Stir in water.

Pour mixture into freezer can of a 1-gallon hand-turned or electric freezer. Freeze according to manufacturer's instructions. Yield: 2 quarts.

Note: Ice may be stored in freezer compartment of refrigerator until serving time. Let stand at room temperature 10 to 15 minutes before serving.

PETITS FOURS

1 cup butter, softened
1 cup sugar
6 eggs
2¼ cups sifted all-purpose
    flour
⅛ teaspoon salt
1 teaspoon vanilla extract
Glaze (recipe follows)
Decorator Frosting

Cream butter; gradually add sugar, beating well. Add eggs, one at a time, beating well after each addition.

Combine flour and salt, stirring well; add to creamed mixture. Stir in vanilla.

Pour batter into 2 waxed paper-lined, greased, and floured 8-inch square baking pans. Bake at 300° for 40 minutes or until a wooden pick inserted in center comes out clean. Cool in pans 10 minutes; remove from pan, peel off paper, and cool completely on wire racks.

Cut each cake into 1½-inch squares or cut into circles using a 1¾-inch cookie cutter.

Dip individual cakes into glaze. Set on cooling racks to dry. Repeat procedure with remaining glaze to coat cakes well.

Decorate petits fours with Decorator Frosting, using a pastry bag. Yield: 32 square or 28 round petits fours.

Glaze:

7½ cups sifted powdered
    sugar
¼ teaspoon salt
⅔ cup milk
2 teaspoons vanilla extract

Combine all ingredients; beat until smooth. Yield: 3 cups.

Decorator Frosting:

3 egg whites
½ teaspoon cream of tartar
4½ cups sifted powdered
    sugar

Combine egg whites (at room temperature) and cream of tartar in a large mixing bowl. Beat at medium speed of electric mixer until frothy. Gradually add sugar; beat well. Beat 5 to 7 minutes or until frosting is stiff. Yield: about 2 cups.

Note: Paste food coloring may be added to tint frosting to desired shades. Frosting dries quickly; keep container covered with a damp towel.

Léon J. Frémaux. Characters of New Orleans, 1876

New Orleans ice cream vendor painted by Léon J. Frémaux.

A colorful 1913 menu cover for "The Gem" restaurant, when it was located on Royal Street in the Vieux Carré of New Orleans, Louisiana.

CHEESE WAFERS

1 cup butter or margarine, softened
2 cups (8 ounces) shredded sharp Cheddar cheese
1 tablespoon chopped chives
1 teaspoon caraway seeds
½ teaspoon dry mustard
⅛ teaspoon red pepper
2¾ cups all-purpose flour

Cream butter and cheese. Add chives, caraway seeds, mustard, and red pepper; mix well. Gradually stir in flour, blending well. Shape dough into 4 rolls, 1½ inches in diameter. Wrap each roll in waxed paper. Chill at least 3 hours.

Cut rolls into ¼-inch-thick slices, and place on ungreased baking sheets. Bake at 350° for 15 minutes. Remove from baking sheets immediately, and place on wire racks to cool. Yield: about 8 dozen.

PLAIN SYRUP

16 cups sugar
12 cups water

Combine sugar and water in a large Dutch oven. Cook over medium heat, stirring frequently, until mixture comes to a boil. Cook, stirring frequently, until mixture reaches 220°. Remove from heat; cool completely. Store in glass containers. Yield: about 1 gallon.

Ice-shaver from a 1915 catalogue of kitchen utensils.

GRAPE SYRUP

8 cups Plain Syrup
2 cups grape juice
½ cup Burgundy or other dry red wine
Finely crushed ice

Combine Plain Syrup and grape juice in a saucepan; bring to a boil. Reduce heat, and simmer 5 minutes. Remove from heat, and stir in wine. Store in an airtight glass container.

For each serving, place about 1 cup Grape Syrup in a glass. Add enough finely crushed ice to fill glass; stir gently. Yield: about 10 servings.

BANANA SYRUP

10 ripe bananas, mashed
8 cups Plain Syrup
1 tablespoon banana extract
1 tablespoon lemon juice
Finely crushed ice

Cover bananas; let stand in a cool place for 36 hours. Strain through cheesecloth. Combine banana juice and Plain Syrup in a saucepan; bring to a boil. Reduce heat, and simmer 5 minutes. Remove from heat, and stir in banana extract and lemon juice. Store in an airtight glass container.

For each serving, place about 1 cup Banana Syrup in a glass. Add enough finely crushed ice to fill glass; stir gently. Yield: about 10 servings.

FOR SPECIAL GUESTS

Dinners for Preachers to Presidents

Southerners love company; we always have. From the tables of working farmers who grow almost every bite the family eats, to the elegant public dining rooms at places like the Park Avenue Room at the Skirvin Plaza Hotel in Oklahoma, we learn that the love of good food is common to us all. But sharing that food is what makes us happiest.

It is not the expense that makes it taste good; of that we may be sure. It can be a spring chicken freshly dressed from a Tennessee barnlot, endangered species that it is, or a two and a half-inch thick steak at the Pitchfork Ranch in Texas; it is the welcome, the camaraderie that makes a feast.

Over a period of some two hundred years, some interesting food-related affairs have fallen out of use. Time has eroded their places in society. One was the Gentlemen's Club of the East coast. Men of means, basing their clubs on the English tradition, met regularly to solve the problems of the day, drink, smoke their pipes, and end with a light supper around ten. One club had a rule that "no fresh liquor shall be made, prepared or produced after 11 o'clock at night."

Another chapter of Southern history closed with the obsolescence of the Fredericksburg Sunday House. German immigrants settled the hill country of Gillespie County, Texas, around 1846. Living miles apart, they contrived a unique way of congregating in their town of Fredericksburg. They built simple one- or two-room houses, most of them near churches, to live in on weekends. Families tucked themselves into wagons, and later into cars, and spent weekends carrying on their traditional singing and debating societies, shopping, and attending church. Feasting and fellowship helped them overcome memories of the dreadful hardships they had suffered in establishing themselves in this country.

But what's a songfest without beer? Charles H. Nimitz built the town's first hotel in 1852. It only had four rooms, but it had a brewery. As years passed, the Nimitz grew to forty-five rooms and its dining room was said to be the finest on the frontier.

Sunday is our turn to feed the preacher. Do you really think two meats and two desserts will be enough?

COMPANY *IS* COMING!

ompany's here! You open the door, your guests hesitate, breathe in the aroma of herbs and roast capon, and somebody's bound to ask, "Whose birthday is it?" The combination clicks every time. Reposing, plump and golden, on a platter and surrounded by a colorful melange of vegetables, capon is as noble as an entree can be. In such a dinner, each element plays a part, and this bird will be remembered as well for the company it keeps. Burnish the silver, unwrap the best linen, and enjoy!

OVEN-ROASTED CAPON
PARSLEY POTATO MEDLEY
CAPON GRAVY
FRESH GREEN BEANS
PINEAPPLE CHEDDAR SALAD
SLICED TOMATO & SWEET PICKLE PLATTER
COMPANY'S COMING BISCUITS
OLD-TIME APPLE PIE

Serves 8

OVEN-ROASTED CAPON

1 (7- to 8-pound) capon
1 teaspoon dried parsley flakes
¾ teaspoon dried whole thyme
½ teaspoon rubbed sage
¼ teaspoon salt
⅛ teaspoon freshly ground pepper
Vegetable oil

Remove giblets and neck from capon; reserve for other uses. Rinse capon with cold water; pat dry. Combine herbs and seasonings; rub on surface and in cavity of capon. Fold neck skin over back; secure with a wooden pick. Lift wingtips up and over back so they are tucked under capon securely. Place capon, breast side up, in a shallow roasting pan; cover, and refrigerate overnight.

Brush capon with oil. Insert meat thermometer in breast or meaty part of thigh, making sure it does not touch bone. Bake at 325° for 2½ hours or until meat thermometer registers 185°. Baste capon frequently with pan drippings. If capon gets too brown, cover lightly with aluminum foil. Capon is done when legs move easily.

Transfer capon to serving platter; reserve pan drippings for Parsley Potato Medley and Capon Gravy. Let capon stand 20 minutes before carving. Yield: 8 servings.

PARSLEY POTATO MEDLEY

2½ pounds new potatoes
1½ pounds baby carrots, scraped
3 (10¾-ounce) cans chicken broth
½ cup capon pan drippings
½ cup chopped celery leaves
½ teaspoon salt
½ teaspoon pepper
¼ teaspoon dried whole rosemary
⅓ cup chopped fresh parsley

Combine all ingredients, except parsley, in a large Dutch oven. Bring to a boil; reduce heat, and cook over medium heat 35 minutes or until vegetables are tender. Drain. Cool slightly, and peel potatoes. Sprinkle vegetables with parsley. Yield: 8 servings.

CAPON GRAVY

¼ cup plus 2 tablespoons all-purpose flour
¼ cup plus 2 tablespoons capon pan drippings
2 cups milk
Salt and pepper to taste

Brown flour in a skillet over medium heat; stir in pan drippings to form a smooth paste. Gradually add milk. Cook, stirring constantly, until thickened and bubbly. Season to taste with salt and pepper. Serve as a side dish. Yield: 2¼ cups.

Oven-Roasted Capon with Parsley Potato Medley, Capon Gravy in serving boat, Fresh Green Beans, Old-Time Apple Pie, and Company's Coming Biscuits.

FRESH GREEN BEANS

2 pounds fresh green beans
6 cups water
1 (¼-pound) ham hock
1 teaspoon salt
Dash of sugar

Remove ends from green beans, and cut diagonally into 2-inch pieces. Wash beans.

Place water and ham hock in a Dutch oven; bring to a boil. Reduce heat; cover and simmer 10 minutes. Add beans, salt, and sugar; cover, and cook 20 minutes or until tender. Yield: 8 servings.

Note: For Southern-style green beans, cook over low heat about 2 hours or until very tender.

PINEAPPLE CHEDDAR SALAD

1 (3-ounce) package lemon-flavored gelatin
1 cup boiling water
1 (8¼-ounce) can crushed pineapple, undrained
¾ cup sugar
1 cup whipping cream, whipped
1 cup (4 ounces) shredded mild Cheddar cheese
½ cup chopped pecans (optional)

Dissolve gelatin in water. Stir in pineapple and sugar; cool. Fold in whipped cream and cheese; add pecans, if desired. Spoon into a lightly oiled 9-inch square pan; chill until firm. Cut into squares to serve. Yield: 9 servings.

COMPANY'S COMING BISCUITS

2 cups all-purpose flour
1 tablespoon baking powder
2 teaspoons sugar
½ teaspoon salt
½ teaspoon baking soda
½ teaspoon cream of tartar
½ cup shortening
¾ cup plus 2 tablespoons buttermilk

Sift together dry ingredients. Cut in shortening with pastry blender until mixture resembles coarse meal. Sprinkle buttermilk evenly over flour mixture, stirring until dry ingredients are moistened. Turn dough out onto a lightly floured surface; knead 3 to 5 times until smooth.

Roll dough out to ½-inch thickness; cut with a 2½-inch biscuit cutter. Place biscuits on a lightly greased baking sheet. Bake at 450° for 10 to 12 minutes or until lightly browned. Yield: about 1 dozen.

OLD-TIME APPLE PIE

Lattice-Crust Pastry
6 medium-size cooking apples, peeled, cored, and thinly sliced
⅔ cup plus 2 tablespoons sugar
¼ cup firmly packed brown sugar
½ cup orange juice
1 cup water
½ teaspoon ground nutmeg
½ teaspoon ground cinnamon
2 tablespoons butter or margarine
1 egg white, beaten

Roll half of pastry to ⅛-inch thickness; line a 9-inch pie-plate.

Combine apples, ⅔ cup sugar, brown sugar, orange juice, and water in a medium saucepan; bring to a boil. Reduce heat; cover, and simmer 5 minutes or until apples are tender.

Drain apples, and set aside. Reserve syrup in saucepan; cook over medium heat until volume is reduced by half. Add spices, stirring well.

Spoon apples into pastry-lined pieplate. Pour syrup (about ½ cup) over apples, and dot with butter.

Roll out remaining pastry to ⅛-inch thickness, and cut into fourteen 10- x ½-inch strips. Arrange strips in lattice design over pie; press ends gently to seal strips to pastry overhang. Brush with egg white, and sprinkle with remaining sugar. Bake at 450° for 10 minutes; reduce heat to 350°; bake 30 minutes or until lightly browned. Yield: one 9-inch pie.

Lattice-Crust Pastry:

2 cups all-purpose flour
½ teaspoon salt
⅔ cup plus 2 tablespoons shortening
5 to 6 tablespoons cold water

Combine flour and salt; cut in shortening with pastry blender until mixture resembles coarse meal. Sprinkle cold water evenly over surface; stir with a fork until dry ingredients are moistened. Shape dough into a ball; chill. Yield: pastry for one 9-inch lattice-crust pie.

Label from pineapple can, c.1900

FREDERICKSBURG SUNDAY HOUSE DINNER

The Sunday House was, so far as is known, unique to turn-of-the-century Fredericksburg, Texas. Farmers and ranchers from outlying districts came into town on weekends to enjoy shopping, dances, and worship services. At first, they camped under the trees, but the one-room hut soon appeared. Then came two-room cabins of log or stone, the second room on top of the first, with an outside stair.

Sunday dinner was often quite sumptuous and was followed by an afternoon of cards and visiting. The houses were then locked up until the family's next weekend in town. However, the houses also became emergency living quarters when illness struck a ranch family, and they needed medical attention in town.

BAKED CHICKEN * BREADCRUMB DRESSING
HOMEMADE EGG NOODLES
WINTER GREEN BEAN SALAD
or
SUMMER FRUIT COMBINATION
POPPY SEED CAKE

Serves 6

BAKED CHICKEN

1 (4- to 5-pound) baking hen
Vegetable oil

Remove giblets and neck from cavity of chicken, and reserve for dressing. Rinse chicken with cold water, and pat dry. Rub skin well with oil. Place chicken, breast side up, in a roasting pan. Bake, uncovered, at 375° for 2 hours; baste chicken frequently with pan juices. Serve with Breadcrumb Dressing. Yield: 6 servings.

BREADCRUMB DRESSING

Giblets and neck of baking hen
5½ cups water
1 cup finely chopped celery
3 tablespoons butter or margarine, melted
2 cups cornmeal
4 cups soft breadcrumbs
3 eggs, beaten
1 tablespoon minced onion
1 teaspoon salt
½ teaspoon pepper
⅛ teaspoon sage (optional)

Combine giblets, neck, and water in a large saucepan. Cook 30 minutes. Drain, reserving 3½ cups broth. Discard giblets and neck.

Sauté celery in butter until tender. Combine celery, remaining ingredients, and reserved broth in a large mixing bowl; stir until well blended.

Spoon mixture into a well-greased 9-inch square baking pan. Bake at 350° for 40 to 45 minutes. Yield: 6 servings.

HOMEMADE EGG NOODLES

2½ cups all-purpose flour
4 eggs
2 tablespoons milk
4 quarts water
1½ teaspoon salt
1 tablespoon vegetable oil
1 cup toasted bread cubes
2 tablespoons butter or margarine, melted

Make a well in center of flour. Break 1 whole egg in well; draw part of flour into egg, using the fingertips of one hand. Repeat procedure with remaining eggs. Add milk, and stir well. Turn dough out on lightly floured surface; knead 10 minutes.

Shape dough into a ball, and place in a container; cover tightly. Let rest in refrigerator 1 hour.

Roll dough out to 1/16-inch thickness on a lightly floured surface, stretching with each roll. Hang dough up to dry about 30 minutes. Roll into a scroll, and cut in ¼- to ½-inch slices. Unroll, and hang up until completely dry.

Combine water, salt, and oil in a large Dutch oven; bring to a boil. Add noodles, and cook 10 minutes or until noodles are tender. Drain well.

Combine toasted bread cubes and butter, tossing lightly; sprinkle over noodles. Yield: 4 to 6 servings.

University of Texas, Austin

Above: A roundup in Ward County, Texas, 1897.
Below: One of the few remaining rock Sunday Houses,
unique to Texas frontier.

WINTER GREEN BEAN SALAD

2 (16-ounce) cans
   French-style green beans,
   drained
6 slices bacon, cooked and
   crumbled
1 small onion, chopped
⅓ cup vinegar
⅓ cup sugar
1 teaspoon salt
½ teaspoon pepper

Combine beans, bacon, and onion in a large bowl, tossing lightly.

Combine remaining ingredients, mixing well. Pour over vegetables, stirring gently to blend well. Cover, and refrigerate 24 hours. Yield: 6 servings.

Barry A. Smith

POPPY SEED CAKE

2 cups milk, scalded
½ cup poppy seeds
1 cup butter or margarine, softened
2½ cups sugar
4 cups sifted cake flour
1 tablespoon plus 1 teaspoon baking powder
½ teaspoon salt
1 tablespoon vanilla extract
5 egg whites
Filling (recipe follows)

Combine milk and poppy seeds. Cover, and let stand overnight in refrigerator.

Cream butter; gradually add sugar, beating well.

Combine flour, baking powder, and salt; add to creamed mixture alternately with milk mixture, beginning and ending with flour mixture. Mix well after each addition. Stir vanilla into batter.

Beat egg whites (at room temperature) until stiff peaks form; fold into creamed mixture.

Pour batter into 4 greased and floured 9-inch round cakepans. Bake at 350° for 25 minutes or until a wooden pick inserted in center comes out clean. Cool in pans 10 minutes; remove layers from pans, and cool completely. Spread filling between layers and on top of cake. Yield: one 4-layer cake.

Filling:

¼ cup plus 1½ teaspoons all-purpose flour
4 cups milk
2 cups sugar
5 egg yolks
1 teaspoon vanilla extract
1 cup chopped pecans

Combine first 4 ingredients in a heavy saucepan; stir until well blended. Cook over medium heat until thickened. Stir in vanilla and pecans. Cool. Yield: about 4 cups.

Fresh summer fruit with sweet, spicy dressing.

SUMMER FRUIT COMBINATION

4 bananas, cut into ½-inch slices
2 oranges, peeled and sliced crosswise
½ fresh pineapple, peeled, cored, and cut into spears
½ cantaloupe, cut into ½-inch slices
¼ small watermelon, cut into wedges
1 cup fresh blueberries
1 cup seedless green grapes
½ cup sliced fresh strawberries
1 (3-ounce) package cream cheese, cut into ½-inch cubes
Leaf lettuce
Dressing (recipe follows)

Arrange fruit and cream cheese attractively on a lettuce-lined serving platter. Serve with dressing. Yield: 8 servings.

Dressing:

1½ cups vegetable oil
½ cup sugar
¼ cup plus 2 tablespoons vinegar
1½ tablespoons poppy seeds
1½ teaspoons grated onion
1½ teaspoons salt
1½ teaspoons dry mustard
1½ teaspoons paprika

Combine all ingredients in a jar. Cover tightly, and shake vigorously. Yield: about 1¾ cups.

PICKED FOR THE PREACHER

I n rural communities, where church congregations were too small to support a full-time pastor, a preacher kept to a schedule of visiting, one Sunday a month, each of his ministries. On their appointed Sunday, the worshipers turned out, almost to a man. Women parishioners vied with one another to "feed the preacher." Like this: "My mother . . . prepared for Second Sunday preaching by taking to the kitchen for prodigious feats of stewing and baking and frying on the off-chance that Brother Webber, the circuit riding Methodist minister, would come to our house for dinner."

BARBECUED POT ROAST
STEAMED CHICKEN AND GRAVY
BAKED RICE
LADY PEAS
or
BLACK-EYED PEAS
SCALLOPED EGGPLANT ∗ FRIED OKRA
RELISH BOWL ∗ FRESH SLICED TOMATOES
CORNMEAL CRISPS
DOWN HOME BISCUITS
SWEET POTATO CUSTARD PIE
or
BANANA PUDDING

Serves 6 to 8

BARBECUED POT ROAST

1 (4- to 5-pound) boneless pot roast
2 tablespoons vegetable oil
1½ cups sliced onions
1 clove garlic, minced
2 teaspoons salt
½ teaspoon pepper
1 (8-ounce) can tomato sauce
¼ cup chili sauce
⅓ cup cider vinegar
2 tablespoons firmly packed brown sugar
2 teaspoons Worcestershire sauce
½ cup water
2 teaspoons chili powder
8 new potatoes
3 carrots, peeled and cut into strips

Brown roast on both sides in hot oil in a large Dutch oven. Add onion and garlic; cook until onion is tender.

Combine salt, pepper, and tomato sauce; pour over roast, and cook over low heat, uncovered, 1½ hours. Combine next 6 ingredients; pour over roast. Cook over low heat, covered, 1 hour or until tender.

Pare 1-inch strip around center of potatoes. Add potatoes and carrots during last 30 minutes of cooking time. Transfer roast to serving platter, and serve with vegetables. Yield: 8 to 10 servings.

STEAMED CHICKEN AND GRAVY

2 (1¾-to 2-pound) split broiler-fryers
1 teaspoon salt
1 teaspoon pepper
Vegetable oil
2 cups water
¼ cup butter or margarine
2 tablespoons all-purpose flour
¼ cup water

Sprinkle chicken with salt and pepper, and cook in ⅛-inch hot oil (375°) until lightly brown. Place chicken in a large Dutch oven; add water and butter. Cook, covered, over medium heat for 40 minutes or until tender.

Remove chicken to serving platter; reserve pan drippings. Combine flour and ¼ cup water; stir until smooth. Pour flour mixture into pan drippings; cook, stirring constantly, until thickened and bubbly. Serve gravy with chicken and Baked Rice. Yield: 6 to 8 servings.

Dinner for the visiting preacher features Barbecued Pot Roast and Steamed Chicken with Gravy accompanied by Relish Platter, Scalloped Eggplant, Down Home Biscuits, Lady Peas and a favorite Southern dessert, Banana Pudding.

BAKED RICE

2 tablespoons vegetable oil
1 cup uncooked regular rice
¼ cup chopped onion
2 cups chicken broth, undiluted
1 tablespoon butter or margarine
¾ cup fresh mushrooms, sliced
¼ teaspoon salt

Heat oil in a large cast-iron skillet; add rice and onion. Cook over medium heat until rice is lightly browned. Add chicken broth; stir well.

Melt butter in a small skillet. Sauté mushrooms in butter about 5 minutes. Stir into rice mixture. Add salt; stir well.

Cover, and bake at 350° for 30 minutes. Yield: 8 servings.

LADY PEAS

3½ cups fresh lady peas
2 cups water
¼ pound salt pork, cut into ½-inch cubes
Salt to taste

Combine all ingredients in a 2-quart saucepan; bring to a boil. Reduce heat; cover, and simmer 30 minutes or until peas are tender. Add more water, if needed, to keep peas from sticking to the pan. Yield: 6 to 8 servings.

BLACK-EYED PEAS

3 cups water
4 cups shelled fresh black-eyed peas
1 (¾-pound) ham hock
1 medium onion, chopped
½ teaspoon salt
¼ teaspoon pepper

Combine all ingredients in a 3-quart Dutch oven; bring to a boil. Reduce heat; cover, and simmer 30 minutes or until peas are tender. Add more water, if needed, to keep peas from sticking to the pan. Yield: 6 to 8 servings.

SCALLOPED EGGPLANT

2 medium eggplants, peeled and diced
2 medium onions, chopped
⅔ cup chopped green pepper
¼ cup plus 2 tablespoons bacon drippings
1 pound ground beef
1 tablespoon salt
2 teaspoons sugar
¼ teaspoon pepper
4 cups soft bread crumbs
1½ cups (6 ounces) shredded sharp Cheddar cheese
2 (10¾-ounce) cans tomato puree

Cover eggplant with boiling water; let stand 5 minutes. Drain; set aside.

Sauté onion and green pepper in bacon drippings in a large skillet. Add ground beef, and cook until browned; stir to crumble. Drain off all of pan drippings.

Add eggplant and remaining ingredients; spoon into a greased, shallow 2-quart baking dish. Bake, covered, at 350° for 30 minutes. Remove cover, and bake 10 minutes or until brown. Yield: 8 servings.

FRIED OKRA

3 pounds okra
5 slices bacon
½ teaspoon salt
¼ teaspoon pepper

Wash okra well; drain. Cut off tip and stem ends; cut okra into ¼-inch slices, and set aside.

Cook bacon in a large skillet until crisp; remove bacon, reserving drippings in skillet. Crumble bacon, and set aside.

Sprinkle salt and pepper over okra; toss gently. Cook okra in reserved bacon drippings over medium heat 30 minutes, stirring frequently. Cover, and cook an additional 15 minutes or until okra is tender, stirring occasionally. Yield: 6 to 8 servings.

Note: This is a traditional method of frying okra without batter.

CORNMEAL CRISPS

1¼ cups boiling water
¾ cup cornmeal
2 tablespoons shortening, melted
¾ teaspoon salt

Pour water over cornmeal, stirring constantly. Add shortening and salt, mixing well. Drop by tablespoonfuls onto lightly greased baking sheets (the mixture will be thin). Bake at 425° for 25 minutes or until brown and crisp. Yield: 1½ dozen 3-inch crisps.

DOWN HOME BISCUITS

4 cups all-purpose flour
2 tablespoons plus 2 teaspoons baking powder
1 tablespoon plus 1 teaspoon sugar
2 teaspoons salt
⅔ cup shortening
1½ to 1¾ cups buttermilk

Sift dry ingredients; cut in shortening until mixture resembles coarse meal. Sprinkle buttermilk evenly over flour mixture, stirring until ingredients are moistened. Turn dough out onto a lightly floured surface; knead lightly 4 to 5 times.

Pat dough out to ½-inch thickness; cut with a 2½-inch biscuit cutter. Place biscuits on a lightly greased baking sheet. Bake at 450° for 10 to 12 minutes or until lightly browned. Yield: about 2 dozen.

Pioneers entertaining Father Kennedy, Palm Beach, 1900.

SWEET POTATO CUSTARD PIE

3 eggs, separated
¾ cup sugar
1 cup hot cooked, mashed
   sweet potatoes
¼ cup butter or margarine
1½ cups milk
1 teaspoon vanilla extract
½ teaspoon ground cinnamon
½ teaspoon ground nutmeg
1 unbaked 10-inch pastry
   shell

Beat yolks until thick. Gradually add sugar; mix well. Add next 6 ingredients; mix well.

Beat egg whites (at room temperature) until stiff peaks form; fold into sweet potato mixture. Pour into pastry shell, and bake at 350° for 50 minutes or until set. Yield: one 10-inch pie.

BANANA PUDDING

1½ cups sugar, divided
¼ cup plus 1 teaspoon
   all-purpose flour
3 cups milk, scalded
4 eggs, separated
2 teaspoons vanilla
   extract
60 vanilla wafers
6 bananas, sliced

Combine 1 cup plus 2 tablespoons sugar and flour in top of a double boiler; add milk, and place over boiling water. Cook, stirring constantly, until thickened. Cover, and cook 15 minutes. Add egg yolks; cook 2 minutes, stirring constantly. Remove from heat, and stir in vanilla.

Arrange half of vanilla wafers in a lightly greased 13- x 9- x 2-inch baking dish; top with half of bananas and half of pudding. Repeat layers.

Beat egg whites (at room temperature) until soft peaks form. Gradually add remaining sugar to egg whites, 1 tablespoon at a time, beating until stiff peaks form. Spread meringue over top of pudding mixture, sealing to edge of dish. Bake at 350° for 10 minutes or until golden brown. Yield: 8 servings.

A TASTE OF NEIMAN-MARCUS' PAST

There is hardly a restaurant in the world that can drop more famous names than the Zodiac Room of Neiman-Marcus, Dallas: Coco Chanel, Amy Vanderbilt, the Duke of Windsor, Lord Louis Mountbatten, Princess Grace of Monaco, President and Mrs. Lyndon B. Johnson, for example. The late Helen Corbitt, one of the most original food persons of our time, ran the Zodiac from 1955 to 1969. She honored notable customers by creating exquisite menus for them. In 1978 many of Mrs. Corbitt's recipes were compiled in her honor; a sampling follows.

MIMOSA CHAMPAGNE COCKTAIL
CHICKEN VELVET SOUP
VEAL PEDERNALES WITH
GLAZED APPLES
AVOCADO MOUSSE * CHICKEN SALAD
OUR FAMOUS POPOVERS
SOUFFLÉ OF CARAMEL

Serves 6

MIMOSA CHAMPAGNE COCKTAIL

1 pint freshly squeezed
  orange juice, chilled
½ (25.4-ounce) bottle Brut
  champagne, chilled
1 pint lemon sherbet
Fresh mint leaves

Combine orange juice and champagne, stirring gently. Pour into frosted stemmed glasses.

Add 1 scoop lemon sherbet to each glass. Garnish with mint leaves, and serve immediately. Yield: 6 servings.

CHICKEN VELVET SOUP

⅓ cup plus 1 tablespoon
  butter or margarine
¾ cup all-purpose flour
6 cups chicken broth, divided
1 cup milk
1 cup half-and-half
½ teaspoon salt
½ teaspoon pepper
1½ cups chopped cooked
  chicken

Melt butter in a large Dutch oven over low heat; add flour, stirring until smooth. Cook 1 minute, stirring constantly. Gradually add 2 cups chicken broth, milk, and half-and-half. Cook over medium heat, stirring constantly, until thickened and bubbly. Stir in salt and pepper. Add remaining chicken broth and chicken, stirring well. Heat thoroughly. Yield: 2 quarts.

VEAL PEDERNALES WITH GLAZED APPLES

2 pounds (½-inch thick) veal
  cutlets
1 cup all-purpose flour
2 teaspoons salt
½ cup butter or margarine,
  melted
¼ cup olive oil
1 cup chicken broth
3 tablespoons lemon juice
2 lemons, thinly sliced
½ cup fresh parsley, chopped
Lemon slices (optional)
Glazed Apples

Flatten cutlets to ¼-inch thickness, using a meat mallet or rolling pin.

Combine flour and salt; dredge cutlets in flour mixture. Sauté cutlets in butter and olive oil 3 minutes on each side or until browned. Pour chicken broth over the cutlets; reduce heat, and simmer until liquid is reduced by half. Add lemon juice and slices. Continue cooking 5 minutes; remove from heat. Stir in chopped parsley. Transfer cutlets to a serving platter, and pour sauce over top. Garnish with lemon slices, if desired, and serve with Glazed Apples. Yield: 6 to 8 servings.

Glazed Apples:

3 cups sugar
1½ cups water
⅛ teaspoon ground
  cinnamon
6 medium apples, peeled and
  cut into quarters

Combine sugar and water in a small Dutch oven; bring to a boil, and boil 10 minutes. Reduce heat; add cinnamon and apples, stirring gently.

Simmer, uncovered, 30 minutes. Cover, and simmer an additional 20 mintues or until apples are tender and appear transparent.

To serve, transfer to a buttered 1-quart casserole. Yield: 6 servings.

Collection of Bonnie Slotnick

AVOCADO MOUSSE

1 tablespoon unflavored
gelatin
2 tablespoons cold water
1 (3-ounce) package
lime-flavored gelatin
2 cups boiling water
1 cup mashed ripe avocado
½ cup mayonnaise
½ cup whipping cream,
whipped
Lettuce leaves
Chicken Salad

Dissolve unflavored gelatin in
cold water; stir well. Dissolve
lime-flavored gelatin in boiling
water; stir well. Combine gelatin
mixtures, stirring well; chill
until consistency of unbeaten
egg white.

Combine avocado, mayon-
naise, and whipped cream;
gently fold·into gelatin. Pour
into a lightly oiled 4½-cup ring
mold; chill until firm.

Unmold on lettuce leaves, and
fill center with Chicken Salad.
Yield: 6 to 8 servings.

CHICKEN SALAD

2 cups diced cooked chicken
1 cup diced celery
1 cup mayonnaise
Salt to taste
¼ teaspoon white pepper
2 tablespoons sliced almonds,
toasted

Combine first 5 ingredients;
stir gently. Cover; chill 2 hours.
Spoon salad in center of Avocado Mousse, and sprinkle with
almonds. Yield: 6 to 8 servings.

OUR FAMOUS POPOVERS

3 eggs
1¼ cups warm milk (105°
to 115°)
1¼ cups all-purpose flour
Pinch of salt

Beat eggs until light and
lemon-colored. Add warm milk;
stir well. Add flour and salt, stirring just until blended. Pour
batter into well-greased muffin
pans, filling two-thirds full.
Bake at 450° for 15 minutes. Reduce heat to 350°; bake 5 minutes. Serve immediately. Yield:
about 1½ dozen.

SOUFFLÉ OF CARAMEL

4 cups sugar, divided
¼ cup butter or margarine,
softened
12 egg whites
¼ cup water

Sprinkle 1½ cups sugar
evenly in a 10-inch cast-iron
skillet; place over medium heat.
Caramelize sugar by constantly
stirring with a wooden spoon.
Remove sugar from heat. Immediately coat sides and bottom of
a heavily greased 3-quart baking dish with caramelized
sugar. After cooling, rub with
butter. Set aside.

Beat egg whites (at room temperature) until foamy. Gradually
add 2 cups sugar, 1 tablespoon
at a time, beating until stiff
peaks form. Set aside.

Caramelize remaining ½ cup
sugar; gradually add water, stirring well. Cook over medium
heat, stirring often, until mixture reaches softball stage
(240°). Slowly pour hot caramelized syrup over egg whites,
beating 10 minutes at high
speed of electric mixer. Pour egg
white mixture into prepared
dish. Place soufflé dish within a
larger dish; fill outside dish with
water about half way up sides of
soufflé dish. Bake soufflé in this
hot water bath at 300° for 1
hour. Invert onto a serving platter, and serve immediately.
Yield: 6 servings.

Original Neiman-Marcus store opened in Dallas in 1907.

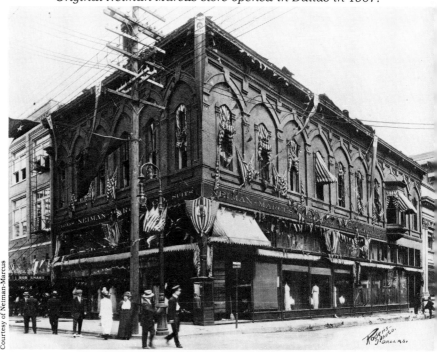

Courtesy of Neiman-Marcus

GENTLEMEN'S SUPPER

"The gentleman of fortune arises about nine o'clock; he perhaps may make an excursion to walk as far as his stables . . . dines between two and three and . . . between nine and ten in the evening he eats a light supper . . . and almost immediately retires to bed." Gentlemen's Clubs flourished among the well-to-do along the Eastern seaboard in the late 1700s and early 1800s. One was The Tuesday Club of Annapolis, whose purpose was unbridled fun. Light entertainment was always enjoyed, but, by the rules, anyone who brought up a serious subject was met by "vociferous and roaring laughter." Before adjourning around eleven o'clock, "at which time no fresh liquor shall be made," they had a light supper.

TOMATO REFRESHER
CRAB ROYAL
CUCUMBER ASPIC
FRENCH BREADSTICKS
TART LEMON MERINGUE PIE

Serves 8

"Mr. Peter Manigault and His Friends . . . " *drawn by Mr. Roupell, c. 1754.*

TOMATO REFRESHER

3 (14½-ounce) cans whole
　tomatoes, undrained
2 cups water
1 thin slice of onion
1 tablespoon butter or
　margarine
2 teaspoons sugar
1 teaspoon salt
12 whole peppercorns
4 whole cloves
1 bay leaf
Fresh parsley sprigs
　(optional)

Combine all ingredients, except parsley, in a medium saucepan; stir well. Bring to a boil; reduce heat, and simmer 20 minutes.

Remove from heat; strain liquid into container, and discard tomatoes, onion, and whole spices. Serve soup hot or cold. Garnish with parsley, if desired. Yield: 4 cups.

CRAB ROYAL

1½ tablespoons minced onion
2 tablespoons minced green
　pepper
3 tablespoons butter or
　margarine
2 tablespoons all-purpose
　flour
1 teaspoon salt
2 cups half-and-half
Dash of ground nutmeg
¼ teaspoon dry mustard
2 egg yolks, beaten
1 (1-pound) can fresh
　crabmeat, drained and
　flaked
Fresh mushrooms (optional)
Fresh parsley sprigs (optional)

Sauté onion and green pepper in butter in a medium skillet until tender. Add flour and salt; stir well. Gradually add half-and-half, stirring until smooth. Add nutmeg and mustard; stir well. Gradually add egg yolks, stirring constantly. Stir in crabmeat; cook over medium heat about 5 minutes. Serve in individual baking shells or dishes, garnishing each with mushrooms and parsley, if desired. Yield: 8 servings.

Crab Royal is the main feature of this light supper.

CUCUMBER ASPIC

2 medium cucumbers, thinly
　sliced
1 (6-ounce) package
　lemon-flavored gelatin
1 (6-ounce) package
　lime-flavored gelatin
4 cups boiling water
⅓ cup white wine vinegar
4 drops green food coloring
¼ teaspoon salt
4 medium cucumbers, peeled,
　seeded, and shredded
½ cup finely chopped celery
2 tablespoons prepared
　horseradish
1 tablespoon grated onion
½ teaspoon dill seeds
Fresh parsley sprigs
2 pints cherry tomatoes
1 (8-ounce) carton
　commercial sour cream
　(optional)

Line a lightly oiled 6½-cup ring mold with cucumber slices. Set aside.

Dissolve gelatin in water; add vinegar, food coloring, and salt, stirring well. Chill until the consistency of unbeaten egg white. Fold in cucumbers, and next four ingredients; spoon into prepared mold. Chill until firm.

Unmold, and garnish with parsley and cherry tomatoes. Serve with sour cream, if desired. Yield: 8 to 10 servings.

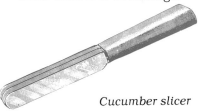

Cucumber slicer

FRENCH BREADSTICKS

1 package dry yeast
2 teaspoons sugar
1¼ cups warm water (105°
  to 115°)
3 to 3½ cups all-purpose
  flour, divided
2 teaspoons salt
Cornmeal
1 egg white
Coarse salt

Dissolve yeast and sugar in water in a large mixing bowl; let stand 5 minutes. Gradually add 1¼ cups flour and salt, beating at low speed of electric mixer until moistened. Increase to high speed, and beat 3 minutes. Gradually add enough remaining flour to make a stiff dough.

Turn dough out onto a heavily floured surface; knead about 5 to 8 minutes, until smooth and elastic. Place dough in a greased bowl, turning to grease top. Cover, and let rise in a warm place (85°), free from drafts, 1 hour or until doubled in bulk. Punch dough down, and turn out onto a lightly floured surface. Knead several times until smooth. Let dough rest for 10 minutes.

Grease two baking sheets; sprinkle with cornmeal, and set aside.

Divide dough into fourths. Clip each fourth into 8 equal portions, using a pair of kitchen shears. Roll each portion into a pencil-like stick 9 inches long. Place sticks about 1 inch apart on prepared baking sheets. Brush lightly with half of egg white. Let rise in a warm place (85°), free from drafts, 30 minutes or until doubled in bulk.

Brush lightly with remaining egg white, and sprinkle with coarse salt. Place a shallow pan containing 1 inch water on bottom rack of oven; place baking sheet on top rack. Bake at 400° for 15 minutes or until golden brown. Yield: 32 breadsticks.

Tart Lemon Meringue Pie: a satisfying end to a light meal.

TART LEMON MERINGUE PIE

1½ cups sugar
¼ cup plus 2 tablespoons
  cornstarch
¼ teaspoon salt
2 cups cold water
½ cup lemon juice
3 eggs, separated
2 tablespoons butter or
  margarine
2 teaspoons grated lemon
  rind
3 to 4 drops yellow food
  coloring
Pastry (recipe follows)
¼ teaspoon cream of tartar
¼ cup plus 2 tablespoons
  sugar

Combine 1½ cups sugar, cornstarch, and salt in a large, heavy saucepan; mix well. Gradually add water and lemon juice, stirring until mixture is smooth.

Beat egg yolks until thick and lemon colored; gradually stir into lemon mixture. Add butter. Cook over medium heat; stir constantly until thickened and bubbly. Cook 1 minute, stirring constantly. Remove from heat; stir in rind and food coloring. Pour into prepared pastry shell.

Combine egg whites (at room temperature) and cream of tartar; beat until foamy. Gradually add remaining sugar, 1 tablespoon at a time, beating until stiff peaks form. Spread meringue over filling, sealing to edge of pastry. Bake at 350° for 12 to 15 minutes or until golden brown. Cool to room temperature. Yield: one 9-inch pie.

Pastry:

1 cup all-purpose flour
½ teaspoon salt
⅓ cup plus 1 tablespoon lard
2 to 3 tablespoons cold water

Combine flour and salt; cut in lard with pastry blender until mixture resembles coarse meal. Sprinkle water evenly over surface; stir with a fork until ingredients are moistened. Shape dough into a ball.

Roll out dough to ⅛-inch thickness on a lightly floured surface. Place in a 9-inch pie-plate; trim off excess pastry around edges. Fold edges under, and flute. Prick bottom and sides of shell with a fork. Bake at 425° for 12 minutes or until golden brown. Yield: one 9-inch pastry shell.

OKLAHOMA ELEGANCE

Oklahoma City's Skirvin Plaza is the hotel that oil built. Big Bill Skirvin made it big in the oil boom, and in 1911 his dream became reality: he built the grandest hotel in the state. He first refused to put rugs in the lobby because the oilmen kept tracking in "black gold." The Neo-Georgian Skirvin, completely restored in 1980, has been the scene of almost every important social and political event in the area since the final brick was laid. The Park Avenue Room was formerly known as the Perle Mesta Room; the "hostess with the mostest" was Big Bill's daughter.

SHRIMP ON ICE
MARINATED ARTICHOKE SALAD
RACK OF LAMB DE SIMONE
BAKED TOMATOES
BAKED POTATO PUFFS
BROCCOLI WITH HOLLANDAISE SAUCE
CRÈME DE MENTHE PARFAITS

Serves 6

SHRIMP ON ICE

1 bunch celery, chopped
1 large onion, chopped
¼ teaspoon ground thyme
12 bay leaves
4 cloves garlic, minced
1 teaspoon red pepper
¼ cup plus 1 tablespoon salt
5 quarts water
5 pounds fresh medium shrimp
4 lemons, quartered
Fresh parsley sprigs (optional)

Combine first 8 ingredients in a stock pot; bring to a boil. Add shrimp, and return to a boil. Lower heat, and simmer 15 to 20 minutes. Drain well; rinse with cold water. Peel and devein shrimp. Serve shrimp with lemon quarters. Garnish with parsley, if desired. Yield: about 6 servings.

Oklahoma City's grand hotel, the Skirvin Plaza, has played host to the world's great, and remains an important role in area society. Skirvin was the father of Washington hostess, Perle Mesta.

SKIRVIN PLAZA

MARINATED ARTICHOKE SALAD

2 (9-ounce) packages frozen artichoke hearts, thawed and drained
1 (4-ounce) jar diced pimiento, drained
½ cup Italian dressing
¼ teaspoon salt
⅛ teaspoon pepper

Place artichokes in a medium bowl. Combine remaining ingredients; pour over artichokes. Toss lightly. Cover, and refrigerate overnight. Yield: 6 servings.

RACK OF LAMB DE SIMONE

4 cups soft breadcrumbs
½ cup butter or margarine, melted
1 tablespoon minced fresh parsley
1 tablespoon olive oil
1 teaspoon salt
½ teaspoon garlic powder
½ teaspoon white pepper
½ teaspoon dried whole basil
3 (1½- to 2-pound) racks of lamb
¼ cup plus 2 tablespoons Dijon mustard
1½ teaspoons dried whole rosemary

Combine first 8 ingredients, mixing well. Set aside.
Place lamb, fat side down, in bottom of shallow roasting pan. Bake at 500° for 8 minutes or until golden brown. Remove from oven, and place lamb, fat side up, in roasting pan.
Combine mustard and rosemary; brush on lamb. Cover lamb with breadcrumb mixture; insert meat thermometer in one of the racks, making sure it does not touch fat or bone.
Reduce heat to 300°; bake lamb until meat thermometer registers 140° (rare), 160° (medium), or 170° (well done). Yield: 6 servings.

BAKED TOMATOES

4 medium tomatoes
¼ cup butter or margarine, melted
1 clove garlic, minced
½ teaspoon salt
½ teaspoon pepper
½ teaspoon dried whole basil
⅛ teaspoon dried whole oregano

Cut tomatoes in ½-inch slices. Place slices in a 13- x 9- x 2-inch baking dish. Combine melted butter and garlic; spoon over tomato slices.
Combine remaining ingredients, and sprinkle over buttered tomato slices. Bake at 350° for 25 minutes. Yield: 6 to 8 servings.

BAKED POTATO PUFFS

4 cups cooked, mashed potatoes
¼ cup butter or margarine, melted
2 egg yolks
½ teaspoon salt
⅛ teaspoon dry mustard
¼ teaspoon pepper
1 egg, beaten

Combine first 6 ingredients; beat on medium speed of an electric mixer until smooth. Shape mixture into 2-inch balls. Flatten balls to ½-inch thickness, and place on a lightly greased baking sheet. Brush surface of each with egg. Bake at 400° for 12 minutes or until browned. Yield: 1½ dozen.

Rack of Lamb de Simone with Baked Tomatoes.

BROCCOLI WITH HOLLANDAISE SAUCE

2 (1-pound) bunches fresh
  broccoli
6 egg yolks
¾ cup butter or margarine,
  softened and divided
1½ tablespoons
  lemon juice
¼ teaspoon salt
Pimiento strips
  (optional)

Trim off large leaves of broccoli. Remove stalks; separate into flowerets, and wash thoroughly. Cook flowerets, covered, in a small amount of boiling water 8 to 10 minutes or until tender. Drain well, and place in a serving bowl. Set aside.

Combine egg yolks and one-third of butter in top of double boiler. Bring water to a boil (water in bottom of double boiler should not touch top pan). Reduce heat to low; cook, stirring constantly, until butter melts. Add second third of butter; stir constantly until butter begins to melt. Add the remaining butter, stirring constantly until melted.

Remove pan from water, and stir rapidly for 2 minutes. Stir in lemon juice, 1 teaspoon at a time; add salt. Place on top of double boiler over low heat. Cook, stirring constantly, 2 to 3 minutes or until smooth and thickened. Immediately remove from heat. Spoon sauce over broccoli, and garnish with pimiento strips, if desired. Yield: 6 servings.

Dining in the style of the Skirvin Plaza.

CRÈME DE MENTHE PARFAITS

1 (8½-ounce) package
  chocolate wafers, crumbled
2 cups whipping cream
¼ cup sifted powdered sugar
¼ cup crème de menthe

Set aside 1 tablespoon chocolate wafer crumbs.

Beat whipping cream at medium speed of an electric mixer until foamy; gradually add sugar, beating until soft peaks form. Pour crème de menthe in a thin stream over whipped cream, beating constantly, until mixture is well blended.

Alternate layers of whipped cream mixture and chocolate wafer crumbs to fill 6 chilled parfait glasses, beginning and ending with whipped cream mixture. Sprinkle reserved crumbs over each parfait to garnish. Serve immediately. Yield: 6 servings.

CATTLE BARONS' STEAK DINNER

In 1953, dignitaries from around the world came to the King Ranch on the Santa Gertrudis to celebrate the 100th anniversary of its beginning. When General Robert E. Lee visited Richard King's spread, Henrietta King served him "viands piled high on a large tin plate, which he de-voured." Much later, Will Rogers wrote that the hospitality of the ranch was as big as its size. General Lee was almost surely treated to a game dinner, while Rogers probably dined on beef. The Kings and other Texas cattle barons developed a style of their own: Welcome! Relax, and come eat!

BROILED STEAKS
BAKED POTATOES
CORN ON THE COB
TOSSED GREEN SALAD WITH CREAMY
BLUE CHEESE DRESSING
SPOON ROLLS
CHERRY PIE

Serves 6

BROILED STEAKS

6 (12-ounce) ribeye steaks, about 1 inch thick
2 tablespoons butter, melted
1 clove garlic, minced
Fresh parsley sprigs (optional)
Radish roses (optional)

Place steaks on rack in broiler pan. Place pan 6 to 7 inches from heat. Broil 6 to 7 minutes on first side; baste with butter and garlic. Turn steaks, and broil second side 6 to 7 minutes, basting with butter and garlic. Place steaks on serving dish, and garnish with parsley and radish roses, if desired. Yield: 6 servings.

BAKED POTATOES

2 tablespoons butter, melted
2 tablespoons vegetable oil
6 medium-size baking potatoes
Kosher salt
6 tablespoons butter or margarine (optional)

Combine butter and oil; set aside.

Scrub potatoes thoroughly, and rub skins with oil mixture; sprinkle with salt. Place in a 13- x 9- x 2-inch baking dish. Bake at 450° for 40 minutes or until done. Slit tops, adding 1 table-spoon butter to each potato, if desired. Yield: 6 servings.

CORN ON THE COB

12 ears of fresh corn, husks and silks removed
½ cup butter or margarine, melted

Place ears of corn in a Dutch oven; cover with cold water. Bring water to a boil. Cover, and remove from heat. Allow corn to remain in the hot water about 5 minutes; drain. Serve with melted butter. Yield: 6 servings.

Variation: Scrape corn off the cob; cook, covered, 15 to 20 minutes. Stir in butter.

Estate of Mrs. Charles J. Belden

Broiled Steak served with Tossed Green Salad and Dressing, Baked Potatoes, Spoon Rolls and Corn. Cherry Pie is the grand finale.

A Texas Longhorn, 1889. Steers turned bleak grazing land into money. Later they worked in movies.

CHERRY PIE

2 (16-ounce) cans pitted tart
  cherries
1 cup sugar
¼ cup all-purpose flour
Lattice-Crust pastry
¼ cup milk
Vanilla ice cream (optional)

Drain cherries, reserving ¾ cup juice. Set cherries aside.

Combine juice, sugar, and flour in a medium saucepan. Cook over medium heat, stirring constantly, until thickened and bubbly. Remove from heat, and stir in cherries.

Spoon filling evenly into pastry shell. Arrange pastry strips in lattice design over filling; seal edges. Pastry strips may be brushed with milk to insure even browning. Bake at 375° for 45 minutes. Serve with vanilla ice cream, if desired. Yield: one 9-inch pie.

Lattice-Crust pastry:

2 cups all-purpose flour
½ teaspoon salt
⅔ cup shortening
5 to 6 tablespoons cold water

Combine flour and salt; cut in shortening until mixture resembles coarse meal. Sprinkle cold water evenly over surface; stir with a fork until all ingredients are moistened. Divide dough in half, and roll each portion to ⅛-inch thickness on a lightly floured surface.

Carefully fit one portion into a 9-inch pieplate and set aside. Cut remaining portion into fourteen ¾-inch-wide strips. Yield: pastry for one lattice crust 9-inch pie.

TOSSED GREEN SALAD

1 small head iceberg lettuce,
  torn
1 small bunch curly endive,
  torn
2 cucumbers, sliced
2 carrots, peeled and grated
3 tomatoes, sliced vertically
1 cup croutons
Creamy Blue Cheese Dressing

Combine lettuce, endive, cucumbers, and carrots in a large bowl; toss gently. Add tomatoes and croutons. Toss gently, and serve with Creamy Blue Cheese Dressing. Yield: 6 servings.

Creamy Blue Cheese Dressing:

¾ cup commercial sour
  cream
3 tablespoons mayonnaise
1 tablespoon lemon juice
¾ teaspoon Worcestershire
  sauce
Tops of 3 green onions,
  chopped
6 ounces blue cheese,
  crumbled
Additional chopped green
  onion (optional)

Combine all ingredients, stirring well. Chill before serving. Garnish with a sprinkling of green onion, if desired. Yield: about 1⅔ cups.

SPOON ROLLS

1 package dry yeast
2 cups warm water (105°
  to 115°)
¾ cup butter or margarine,
  melted
¼ cup sugar
1 egg
4 cups self-rising flour

Dissolve yeast in warm water; set aside.

Combine butter, sugar, and egg in a large mixing bowl; beat until well blended. Add yeast mixture; mix well. Stir in flour to make a soft dough.

Spoon batter into well-greased muffin pans, filling two-thirds full. Bake at 350° for 25 minutes or until lightly browned. Yield: 2 dozen.

Note: Batter may be refrigerated for several days in an airtight container.

AN OCCASIONAL FEAST

The Good Life Through the Years

The first three menus in this chapter are drawn from research into the gastronomic histories of Southern Presidents of the United States: Washington, Jefferson, and Tyler. Two of these great men had more than the presidency and a Virginia background in common: Washington and Jefferson, while insisting on the most lavish outlays of food for their guests, were themselves very abstemious eaters.

Vice President John Tyler acceded to the Presidency on the death of President William Henry Harrison. Letitia Tyler, as First Lady, brought Southern hospitality back to the White House. Two years after Letitia's death, Tyler married the beautiful New York socialite, Julia Gardiner, thirty years his junior. Tyler kept his devotion to mint juleps, champagne, Southern fried quail, and turtle soup, and his young wife added some flourishes of her own. Their entertainments were formidably dressy; some thought Mrs. Tyler rather flamboyant. But when the Whig party turned against him and Tyler was serving out his term as a lame duck, Julia gave a dazzling part for 2,000 guests to prove her husband was not "a man without a party."

Henry Morrison Flagler, the Standard Oil millionaire, fell in love with Florida in 1878 and gambled that the alligator-infested jungle of South Florida could be made into a year-round resort area. Of all his building and developments, Palm Beach intrigued him most. In 1895 Flagler built the Palm Beach Inn, later renamed the Breakers. Jet setters in those days arrived by yacht or private railroad car. At their home, Whitehall, the Flaglers entertained royally . . . and royalty.

Dunleith Mansion, pride of Natchez, with its twenty-six Doric columns, is the house a Northerner sees when he closes his eyes and thinks "Southern." Thistle Hill in Fort Worth was built in 1903 and is a monument to the daring and enterprise of the early Texas cattle barons. Both are listed on the National Register of Historic Places and are steeped in Southern food traditions.

DINING WITH THE WASHINGTONS

A fter attending one of President Washington's official formal Thursday dinners, Pennsylvania Senator William Maclay remembered the menu: "First the soup; fish roasted and boiled; meats, gammon, fowls; etc. . . . Dessert was apple pies, puddings, etc; then iced creams, jellies, etc. . . . then watermelons, muskmelons, apples, peaches, nuts. It was the most solemn dinner I ever was at. . . ." Maclay, a political enemy, found Washington a "cold, formal man." The gammon was probably ham from Mount Vernon, fed on mash from Washington's distillery.

SAVOURY TOMATO SOUP
CREAMED LUMP CRAB ON TOAST POINTS
OLD-FASHIONED ROAST TURKEY * OYSTER DRESSING
CREAMED BRUSSELS SPROUTS AND ONIONS IN
ACORN SQUASH
CREAMY CELERY CASSEROLE
FLOATING ISLANDS * MAIDS OF HONOUR

Serves 8

SAVOURY TOMATO SOUP

1 cup minced leek
2 tablespoons butter or margarine
4 (10½-ounce) cans beef broth, undiluted
1½ cups tomato juice
2 tablespoons sugar
2 tablespoons cornstarch
2½ tablespoons red wine vinegar
2 tablespoons Chablis or other dry white wine
5 large tomatoes, peeled, seeded, and chopped
½ teaspoon salt
¼ teaspoon pepper
Chopped green onion (optional)

Sauté leek in butter until tender and transparent. Add broth, tomato juice, and sugar, stirring well. Bring mixture to a boil; reduce heat, and simmer 10 minutes.

Combine cornstarch, vinegar, and wine, mixing well; stir into tomato juice mixture. Cook, stirring constantly, until slightly thickened. Stir in chopped tomato, salt, and pepper. Serve hot; garnish with chopped green onion, if desired. Yield: about 8 cups.

CREAMED LUMP CRAB ON TOAST POINTS

4 medium-size fresh mushrooms, sliced
¼ cup butter or margarine, melted
1 pound fresh crabmeat, drained and flaked
1 cup whipping cream
2 tablespoons brandy
2 teaspoons chopped fresh parsley
½ teaspoon salt
¼ teaspoon pepper
Toast points

Sauté mushrooms in butter in a large skillet 3 minutes or until tender.

Add next 6 ingredients, stirring gently; heat thoroughly. Serve on toast points. Yield: 8 to 10 servings.

George Washington's soup plate.

Mount Vernon Ladies' Association

J.L.G. Ferris, Archives of 76, Bay Village, Ohio

OLD-FASHIONED ROAST TURKEY

1 (12- to 14-pound) turkey
2 teaspoons salt
½ cup butter or margarine, melted and divided
1 (16-ounce) jar spiced crab apples, drained
Fresh parsley sprigs

Remove giblets and neck from turkey. Rinse turkey thoroughly with cold water; pat dry. Sprinkle salt over surface and in cavity of turkey.

Close cavity of turkey with skewers; tie ends of legs to tail with string or tuck them under flap of skin around tail. Lift wingtips up and over back so that they are tucked under turkey securely.

Brush entire turkey with about ¼ cup melted butter; place breast side up on rack in a roasting pan. Insert meat thermometer in breast or meaty part of thigh, making sure it does not touch bone. Bake at 325° for 5 hours or until meat thermometer registers 190°. Baste turkey frequently with remaining melted butter and pan drippings. If turkey gets too brown during baking, cover lightly with aluminum foil.

When turkey is two-thirds done, cut the cord or band of skin holding the drumstick ends to the tail. This will ensure that the inside of the thighs are thoroughly cooked. Turkey is done when drumsticks are easy to move.

Transfer turkey from roasting pan to serving platter. Let stand 15 minutes before carving. Garnish with crab apples and parsley. Yield: 20 to 24 servings.

OYSTER DRESSING

1 cup chopped celery
1 cup chopped onion
½ cup butter or margarine
2 (12-ounce) containers oysters, drained and chopped
8 cups toasted bread cubes
2 tablespoons chopped fresh parsley
¼ teaspoon poultry seasoning
¼ teaspoon pepper

Sauté celery and onion in butter in a large skillet. Add remaining ingredients; mix well. Spoon mixture into a lightly greased 2-quart casserole. Bake, uncovered, at 400° for 25 minutes. Yield: 8 to 10 servings.

Creamed Brussels Sprouts and Onions in Acorn Squash.

CREAMED BRUSSELS SPROUTS AND ONIONS IN ACORN SQUASH

4 medium acorn squash
3 tablespoons butter or
  margarine, melted
1 teaspoon salt
½ teaspoon pepper
2 (10-ounce) packages frozen
  brussels sprouts
1 pound small white onions
2 tablespoons butter or
  margarine
2 tablespoons all-purpose
  flour
2 cups milk

Cut squash in half lengthwise, and remove seeds. Place cut side down in shallow baking pans, and add 1 inch water. Bake, uncovered, at 400° for 30 minutes or until tender. Drain. Brush inside of hot acorn squash with melted butter; sprinkle with salt and pepper, and set aside.

Combine brussels sprouts and onions; cook according to package directions. Drain, and set aside.

Melt 2 tablespoons butter in a heavy saucepan over low heat. Add flour; cook 1 minute, stirring constantly, until mixture is smooth. Gradually add milk; cook over medium heat, stirring constantly, until thickened and bubbly. Pour white sauce over brussels sprouts and onions; toss gently. Spoon brussels sprouts and onions evenly into squash halves. Yield: 8 servings.

CREAMY CELERY CASSEROLE

3 cups sliced celery
¼ cup plus 2 tablespoons
  butter or margarine, divided
3 tablespoons all-purpose
  flour
1½ cups half-and-half
¾ cup slivered almonds
3 tablespoons fine, dry
  breadcrumbs
Parmesan cheese

Place celery in a medium saucepan; cover with salted water, and lay celery leaves on top. Bring to a boil; cook 10 minutes or until tender. Discard leaves, and drain celery, reserving ¾ cup liquid; set aside.

Melt 3 tablespoons butter in a heavy saucepan over low heat. Add flour; cook 1 minute, stirring constantly, until mixture is smooth. Gradually add half-and-half and celery liquid; cook over medium heat, stirring constantly, until sauce is thickened and bubbly.

Place a layer of celery in a lightly greased 2½-quart casserole. Spoon half the sauce over celery; sprinkle with half the almonds. Repeat layers. Top with breadcrumbs, sprinkle with cheese, and dot with remaining butter. Bake at 350° for 30 minutes. Yield: 8 servings.

Mount Vernon Ladies' Association

Silver coffee pot bearing the Washington coat-of-arms and (above) the Washington family crest.

118

FLOATING ISLANDS

3 egg whites
6 tablespoons sugar
½ teaspoon almond extract
4 cups half-and-half, divided
5 egg yolks
1⅓ cups sugar, divided
¼ teaspoon salt
1 teaspoon vanilla extract
⅓ cup water

Beat egg whites (at room temperature) until soft peaks form; gradually add 6 tablespoons sugar, 1 tablespoon at a time, beating until stiff peaks form. Fold in almond extract.

Heat 3 cups half-and-half in a large skillet to simmering. Shape 8 egg white islands using two spoons; scoop beaten whites onto one spoon and gently place other spoon on top to shape each island. Gently slide the islands into simmering half-and-half. Cook each island two minutes on each side or until slightly firm. Remove islands, and drain on paper towels. Set aside. Reserve half-and-half.

Place yolks in top of a double boiler; beat until thick and lemon colored. Add ⅔ cup sugar and salt, beating well; place over boiling water. Add remaining half-and-half to reserved half-and-half; stir into egg yolk mixture. Cook, stirring constantly, until thickened. Let mixture cool slightly, and stir in vanilla. Chill.

Sprinkle remaining sugar evenly in a 10-inch cast-iron skillet; place over medium heat. Caramelize sugar, stirring constantly with a wooden spoon until light brown and melted. Remove from heat, and add water. Return to heat; cook slowly, stirring constantly, until slightly thickened.

Spoon chilled custard into a serving bowl. Mound islands on top of custard; drizzle caramelized mixture over islands. Serve immediately. Yield: 8 servings.

MAIDS OF HONOUR

1½ cups butter, softened
1 cup sugar
3 egg yolks
3 cups all-purpose flour
¼ teaspoon salt
1½ teaspoons vanilla extract
1 cup strawberry jam
Filling (recipe follows)
Whipped cream (optional)

Cream butter; gradually add sugar, beating until light and fluffy. Add egg yolks, one at a time, mixing well after each addition. Add flour, salt, and vanilla, mixing well.

Shape dough into 1-inch balls; press dough into greased 1¾-inch muffin pans to form shells. Spoon ½ teaspoon jam into each shell. Spoon filling over jam to fill pastry shells.

Bake at 350° for 20 minutes or until set. Remove from pans while warm. Cool. Top each with a dollop of whipped cream, if desired. Yield: 5½ dozen.

Filling:

2 eggs
¾ cup sugar
3 tablespoons dry sherry
1 teaspoon grated lemon rind
¾ cup finely ground almonds
1 tablespoon all-purpose flour
¼ teaspoon salt
¼ teaspoon ground nutmeg
¼ teaspoon ground cinnamon

Beat eggs until light and frothy; gradually add sugar, beating well. Stir in sherry and lemon rind.

Combine almonds, flour, salt, and spices, mixing well. Stir into egg mixture, blending thoroughly. Yield: enough for 5½ dozen pastries.

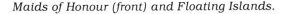

Maids of Honour (front) and Floating Islands.

"TH: JEFFERSON BEGS THE FAVOR . . ."

Massachusetts Congressman Manasseh Cutler recorded this Jeffersonian White House menu in 1802: "Rice soup, round of beef, turkey, mutton, ham, loin of veal, cutlets of mutton, fried eggs, fried beef, and a pie called macaroni." Dessert included "Ice cream, crust wholly dried, crumbled into thin flakes; a dish somewhat like a pudding—inside white as milk . . . covered with cream sauce—very fine. Many other jim-cracks, a great variety of fruit, plenty of wine (and good)."

Jefferson was among the third generation of a prominent Albemarle County, Virginia, family. When he succeeded Benjamin Franklin as Minister to France, he became even more of a Francophile than Franklin, embracing and bringing back many French manners and customs . . . and recipes. Some of the "jim-cracks" Cutler mentioned in passing, perhaps because they were unfamiliar to him, could have been meringues glaće, gâteaux, and soufflés. The ice cream was flavored with vanilla beans, Jefferson's 1791 import from France. "Make mine vanilla" has been heard ever since.

DEVILED EGGS ON WATERCRESS
MONTICELLO GUMBO
STANDING RIB ROAST OF BEEF WITH MADEIRA SAUCE
MACARONI PUDDING
MINTED GREEN PEAS
GARDEN SALAD
BUTTER ROLLS
VANILLA ICE CREAM * MACAROONS
BRANDIED PEACHES * BLANCMANGE

Serves 6 to 8

DEVILED EGGS ON WATERCRESS

4 hard-cooked eggs
2 tablespoons mayonnaise
1 tablespoon capers, drained
4 pitted ripe olives, chopped
2 teaspoons lemon juice
Dash of pepper
Paprika
4 pitted ripe olives, halved
1 bunch of watercress

Slice eggs in half lengthwise, and carefully remove yolks. Mash yolks, and combine with next 5 ingredients. Mix well. Stuff egg whites with yolk mixture. Garnish eggs with paprika and olive halves. Serve on a bed of fresh watercress. Yield: 6 to 8 servings.

Dinner invitation sent by Thomas Jefferson to Captain Cutting, 1793.

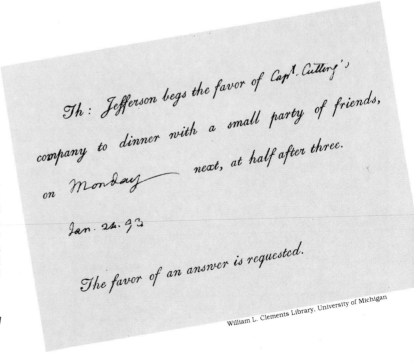

Th: Jefferson begs the favor of Capt. Cutting's company to dinner with a small party of friends, on Monday next, at half after three.

Jan. 24. 93

The favor of an answer is requested.

Standing Rib Roast of Beef with Madeira Sauce, Butter Rolls, and Garden Salad.

MONTICELLO GUMBO

1 pound boneless veal cutlets, cut into 1-inch cubes
½ cup all-purpose flour
¼ cup butter or margarine
1 medium onion, chopped
4 cups sliced okra or 2 (10-ounce) packages frozen cut okra
6 medium tomatoes, peeled and chopped
1 large green pepper, chopped
2 quarts water
2 to 3 teaspoons salt
¼ teaspoon pepper
¼ teaspoon dried parsley flakes
¼ teaspoon dried tarragon
¼ teaspoon dried chives
¼ teaspoon dried chervil
½ teaspoon ground thyme

Dredge veal in flour. Melt butter in large Dutch oven over medium heat; add veal, and cook 1 minute on each side or until lightly browned. Add onion, okra, and tomatoes; cook 15 minutes over low heat. Stir in remaining ingredients; simmer 2 hours, stirring occasionally. Yield: about 2½ quarts.

STANDING RIB ROAST OF BEEF WITH MADEIRA SAUCE

1 (10-pound) standing rib roast
2 teaspoons salt
1 teaspoon ground thyme
1 teaspoon pepper
Fresh parsley sprigs
Whole mushrooms
Madeira Sauce

Trim excess fat from roast, and remove chine. Season roast with salt, thyme, and pepper. Place on rack in a shallow roasting pan. Insert meat thermometer, being careful not to touch bone or fat. Bake, uncovered, at 500° for 10 minutes; reduce temperature to 350°, and bake an additional 2½ to 3 hours or until thermometer reaches 160°. Transfer roast to serving platter. Garnish with parsley and mushrooms. Reserve pan drippings for sauce. Slice and serve immediately with Madeira Sauce. Yield: 6 to 8 servings.

Madeira Sauce:

⅔ cup water
1½ tablespoons butter or margarine
1 tablespoon lemon juice
½ teaspoon salt, divided
½ pound fresh, small mushrooms, sliced
Pan drippings
¼ cup butter or margarine, melted
½ cup chopped green onion
1 cup beef broth
½ cup Madeira wine
1 tablespoon tomato paste
¼ teaspoon pepper

Combine water, 1½ tablespoons butter, and lemon juice. Bring to a boil; reduce heat, and add ¼ teaspoon salt and mushrooms. Cover, and simmer 5 minutes or until mushrooms are tender. Drain, reserving liquid. Set mushrooms aside.

Combine reserved pan drippings, melted butter, and onion; sauté until tender.

Add water to reserved mushroom liquid to equal 1 cup. Combine with onion mixture, broth, wine, tomato paste, pepper, and remaining salt. Heat thoroughly. Stir in mushrooms. Yield: 4 cups.

Tearoom at Thomas Jefferson's Monticello in Virginia.

MACARONI PUDDING

2½ cups uncooked elbow
   macaroni
¼ cup plus 2 tablespoons
   butter or margarine, divided
¼ cup all-purpose flour
2¼ cups milk
½ teaspoon salt
Dash of pepper
3 cups (12 ounces) shredded
   sharp Cheddar cheese

Prepare macaroni according to package directions.

Melt ¼ cup butter over low heat. Add flour; cook 1 minute, stirring constantly until smooth. Gradually add milk; cook over medium heat, stirring constantly, until thickened and bubbly. Stir in salt and pepper.

Place half of macaroni in a lightly greased 3-quart casserole; top with 1 cup cheese. Repeat layers. Pour white sauce over top, and sprinkle with remaining 1 cup cheese. Dot with 2 tablespoons butter. Bake, uncovered, at 400° for 35 to 40 minutes or until lightly browned. Yield: 6 to 8 servings.

MINTED GREEN PEAS

3 pounds fresh green peas
¼ cup butter or margarine,
   melted
2 to 3 fresh mint leaves,
   chopped

Shell and wash peas. Place in a 2-quart saucepan; add salted water to cover. Bring to a boil; reduce heat, and cover. Cook 8 to 12 minutes or until peas are tender; drain.

Combine peas, butter, and mint; toss lightly to coat well. Yield: 6 to 8 servings.

GARDEN SALAD

1 head bibb lettuce, torn
1 small head curly endive,
   torn
1 small head iceberg lettuce,
   torn
1 bunch watercress, torn
½ pound fresh spinach, torn
1 tablespoon chopped
   chives
Vinaigrette Dressing

Combine all ingredients in a large salad bowl; toss lightly. Serve with Vinaigrette Dressing. Yield: 8 servings.

Vinaigrette Dressing:

¾ cup sesame or olive oil
¼ cup plus 2 tablespoons
   tarragon wine winegar
2 tablespoons finely chopped
   green onion
1 teaspoon sugar
¼ teaspoon salt
½ teaspoon dillweed

Combine ingredients in a jar. Cover, and shake vigorously. Chill. Shake well before serving. Yield: 2 cups.

Thomas Jefferson, c. 1799

BUTTER ROLLS

1 cup boiling water
1 cup shortening
1 cup plus ½ teaspoon sugar
1½ teaspoons salt
2 eggs, beaten
2 packages dry yeast
1 cup warm water (105°
   to 115°)
6½ cups all-purpose flour
Melted butter or margarine

Pour boiling water over shortening; stir until shortening is melted. Add 1 cup sugar, salt, and eggs, mixing well. Cool to 105° to 115°.

Dissolve yeast in 1 cup warm water. Add remaining ½ teaspoon sugar, stirring well. Combine shortening mixture and yeast mixture in a large mixing bowl; add flour, stirring until smooth. Cover tightly, and refrigerate overnight.

Remove dough from refrigerator; punch down. Turn dough out onto a lightly floured surface, and knead 3 to 4 times. Divide dough into four portions. Roll each portion into a circle about 12 inches in diameter and ¼-inch thick; cut into 10 wedges. Roll each wedge tightly, beginning at wide end.

Place rolls on greased baking sheets, point side down; curve into crescent shape. Brush tops with melted butter. Cover, and let rise in a warm place (85°), free from drafts, 1½ hours or until doubled in bulk.

Bake at 350° for 20 to 25 minutes or until lightly browned. Yield: about 4 dozen.

VANILLA ICE CREAM

6 egg yolks
1 cup sugar
¼ teaspoon salt
1 quart half-and-half, scalded
3 teaspoons vanilla extract

Beat egg yolks in top of double boiler until thick and lemon colored; gradually add sugar and salt, beating until smooth. Slowly add half-and-half to egg mixture, beating constantly. Place over boiling water, stirring constantly, until custard thickens and coats a spoon. Remove from heat; chill 2 hours.

Pour mixture into freezer can of a 1-gallon hand-turned or electric freezer. Freeze according to manufacturer's instructions. Let ripen 1 hour before serving. Yield: ½ gallon.

MACAROONS

7 (2¼-ounce) packages
   blanched almonds, finely
   chopped
1 tablespoon almond extract
3 egg whites
3 cups sifted powdered sugar

Combine almonds and almond extract. Set aside.

Beat egg whites (at room temperature) until foamy; gradually add sugar, beating until stiff peaks form. Fold in almond mixture. Drop mixture by heaping tablespoonfuls onto unglazed brown paper on cookie sheet. Bake at 300° for 30 minutes or until lightly browned. Remove from paper with spatula while warm. Yield: about 3 dozen.

BRANDIED PEACHES

2 (29-ounce) jars spiced
   peaches, in heavy syrup
12 whole cloves
1 (4-inch) cinnamon stick
⅛ teaspoon ground mace
1 cup brandy

Drain peaches, reserving syrup; set aside. Insert one clove into each peach; place in a medium saucepan. Add reserved syrup, cinnamon, and mace; cook 5 minutes over medium heat. Remove from heat.

Carefully remove peaches from syrup mixture; pack into 3 hot sterilized 1 pint jars, leaving ½-inch headspace. Pour ⅓ cup brandy in each jar. Bring syrup mixture to a boil; reduce heat, and simmer 15 minutes or until mixture is reduced by half.

Pour hot syrup mixture over peaches, leaving ½-inch headspace in jars. Cover at once with metal lids, and screw bands tight. Process in boiling-water bath 20 minutes. Serve over Blancmange or ice cream, if desired. Yield: 3 pints.

BLANCMANGE

1 pound blanched whole
   almonds, finely chopped
1 cup water, divided
1 cup milk
2 tablespoons unflavored
   gelatin
2 cups whipping cream,
   scalded
1 cup sugar
2 tablespoons rum extract
Brandied Peaches (optional)
1 cup whipping cream,
   whipped (optional)

Combine almonds, ½ cup water, and milk. Let stand 15 minutes.

Squeeze almond mixture through a cheesecloth to extract liquid. Discard almonds.

Dissolve gelatin in remaining ½ cup water; set aside.

Combine cream, sugar, and gelatin mixture; stir well to dissolve. Add almond liquid and rum extract; blend well.

Pour mixture into a 5-cup mold. Chill until firm. Serve with Brandied Peaches and whipped cream, if desired. Yield: 8 servings.

SHERWOOD FOREST HOSPITALITY

Our tenth President, John Tyler, was the fourth generation of his family to bear the name and to remember that it was they who gave their Middle Plantation as the site for Williamsburg. Tyler's house, Sherwood Forest, is the longest frame house in America, three hundred feet from one end to the other. His descendants have never left the home, and at Christmas the family still gathers there. The menu follows tradition: First, mint juleps, then the traditional baked Virginia ham, watermelon pickle, candied sweet potatoes, and Sally Lunn or spoon bread. For dessert a wide variety including ambrosia, fruitcake, pound cake, Charlotte Russe, and President Tyler's favorite, Puddin' Pie—a rich coconut custard suitable for tarts or pastry shells, but traditionally referred to as "pudding."

As pictured at left, our somewhat modified menu is served on the china used by President Tyler in the White House.

BAKED VIRGINIA HAM
GREEN BEANS WITH ALMONDS
CANDIED SWEET POTATOES
SPICED PEACHES
PLANTATION SPOON BREAD
BUTTERHORNS
TYLER PUDDING

Serves 8

BAKED VIRGINIA HAM

1 (12- to 15-pound) country
  ham
Whole cloves
2 cups orange juice, divided
About ¾ cup firmly packed
  brown sugar
Fresh parsley sprigs (optional)
Wine Meat Sauce (optional)

Place ham in a very large container; cover with cold water, and soak overnight. Remove ham from water, and drain. Scrub ham thoroughly with a stiff brush, and rinse well with cold water.

Replace ham in container, and cover with fresh cold water. Bring to a boil; reduce heat and simmer, covered, 1 hour. Drain off water.

Cover ham with fresh cold water. Cover and simmer an additional 4 to 5 hours, allowing 25 minutes per pound. Turn ham occasionally during cooking time. Cool.

Carefully remove ham from water; remove skin. Place ham, fat side up, on a cutting board; score fat in a diamond design, and stud with whole cloves. Place ham, fat side up, in a shallow roasting pan. Combine 1 cup orange juice and sugar. Coat exposed portion of ham with orange juice mixture. Bake, uncovered, at 325° for 30 minutes, basting frequently with remaining orange juice. Transfer to serving platter; garnish with parsley, and serve Wine Meat Sauce, if desired, as a side dish. Yield: about 24 to 30 servings.

Wine Meat Sauce:

1 (18-ounce) jar apple jelly
½ cup port wine
¼ teaspoon onion juice
½ teaspoon ground
  ginger
Pinch of pepper

Combine all ingredients in a small saucepan; cook until thoroughly heated. Remove from heat; skim off foam with a metal spoon. Serve with sliced ham. Yield: about 1¼ cups.

GREEN BEANS WITH ALMONDS

3 (10-ounce) packages frozen
  cut green beans or 4 cups
  fresh green beans, cooked
1 cup blanched almonds,
  toasted
¼ cup butter or margarine
½ teaspoon dried whole
  oregano

Cook green beans according to package directions; drain.

Sauté almonds in butter until lightly browned. Add almonds and oregano to cooked green beans, and toss well. Yield: 8 servings.

Note: ½ cup sliced almonds, toasted, may be substituted for blanched almonds.

*Baked Virginia Ham (front),
Candied Sweet Potatoes
(front right), Green Beans
with Almonds (right center),
Butterhorns (left center),
Spiced Peaches (rear).*

Left: Julia Gardiner Tyler our youngest First Lady. Right: Molasses pitcher (late 1800s) from Tyler's Sherwood Forest plantation.

SPICED PEACHES

2 (29-ounce) cans peach
  halves in heavy syrup
2 teaspoons whole cloves
4 (3-inch) cinnamon sticks
1⅓ cups sugar
1 cup vinegar

Drain peach halves, reserving syrup. Combine syrup, cloves, cinnamon sticks, sugar, and vinegar in a medium saucepan. Bring to a boil; cover, and simmer 5 minutes. Remove from heat; add peach halves, and cool completely. Refrigerate in an airtight glass container overnight. Yield: 8 servings.
Note: Flavor of peaches becomes stronger when stored several days.

PLANTATION SPOON BREAD

2 cups cornmeal
2 cups boiling water
1½ cups milk
1 teaspoon salt
¼ cup butter or margarine,
  melted
3 eggs, separated

Combine cornmeal and water; stir until well blended. Mixture will be thick. Stir in milk, salt, and butter.

Beat egg yolks until thick and lemon colored; stir into cornmeal mixture. Beat egg whites (at room temperature) until stiff but not dry; gently fold into cornmeal mixture.

Pour into a lightly greased 1½-quart casserole. Bake at 350° for 40 minutes or until a knife inserted in the center of the bread comes out clean. Yield: 8 servings.

CANDIED SWEET POTATOES

8 large sweet potatoes
1¾ cups firmly packed brown
  sugar
½ cup butter or margarine,
  melted
1½ teaspoons ground
  cinnamon
1 cup chopped pecans
¾ cup water
2 tablespoons grated orange
  rind

Cook sweet potatoes in boiling water to cover 35 to 40 minutes or until tender. Let cool to touch; peel, and cut into ½-inch slices. Combine sugar, butter, cinnamon, and pecans. Arrange a layer of potatoes in a lightly greased 13- x 9- x 2-inch baking pan. Sprinkle half of sugar mixture over potatoes. Repeat layers. Add water, and sprinkle with orange rind. Bake at 350° for 35 minutes. Yield: 8 to 10 servings.

Yam Variation:

½ cup firmly packed brown
  sugar
1 tablespoon cornstarch
1 cup orange juice
¼ cup butter or margarine,
  softened
3 (17-ounce) cans yams

Combine sugar, cornstarch, and orange juice in a small saucepan. Bring to a boil; reduce heat. Cook, stirring constantly, until thickened. Add butter, stirring until melted. Place yams in a 2-quart casserole. Pour glaze over yams. Bake, uncovered, at 350° for 20 minutes. Yield: 8 to 10 servings.

BUTTERHORNS

2 packages dry yeast
1 cup warm water (105°
  to 115°)
6 cups all-purpose flour,
  divided
½ cup sugar
1 teaspoon salt
1¼ cups butter or margarine,
  melted and divided
3 eggs

Dissolve yeast in warm water in a large bowl; let stand 5 minutes. Add 1½ cups flour, sugar, and salt; stir until well blended. Cover, and let rise in a warm place (85°), free from drafts, about 30 minutes or until doubled in bulk.

Add 1 cup melted butter and eggs; stir until blended. Stir in remaining flour to make a soft dough. Turn out onto a lightly floured surface; knead for 10 minutes or until dough is smooth and elastic. Place in a well-greased bowl, turning to grease top. Let rest 15 minutes.

Punch dough down, and divide into three portions. Roll each portion into a circle about 12 inches in diameter and ¼-inch thick; cut into 16 wedges. Brush each wedge with remaining melted butter, and roll tightly, beginning at wide end.

Place rolls on greased baking sheets, point side down; curve into crescent shape. Cover, and let rise in a warm place (85°), free from drafts, 40 minutes or until doubled in bulk. Bake at 425° for 8 to 10 minutes or until lightly browned. Yield: 4 dozen.

TYLER PUDDING

2 tablespoons butter or
  margarine, softened
1¼ cups sugar
2 eggs
¼ cup half-and-half
1½ cups grated fresh coconut
Pastry (recipe follows)

Cream butter; gradually add sugar, beating well. Add eggs, one at a time, beating well after each addition. Stir in half-and-half and coconut. Pour into pastry shell.

Bake at 300° for 55 minutes or until knife inserted comes out clean. Cool before chilling. Yield: one 9-inch pie.

Pastry:

1 cup all-purpose flour
½ teaspoon salt
⅓ cup plus 1 tablespoon
  shortening
2 to 3 tablespoons cold water

Combine flour and salt; cut in shortening with pastry blender until mixture resembles coarse meal. Stir with a fork, adding enough cold water, 1 tablespoon at a time, to moisten. Shape dough into a ball, and chill.

Roll out dough to ⅛-inch thickness on a lightly floured surface. Place in a 9-inch pie-plate; trim off excess pastry. Fold edges under, and flute. Yield: one 9-inch pastry shell.

When President John Tyler, left, married Julia Gardiner, she was a vivacious and queenly New Yorker of twenty-four, thirty years his junior. She so enlivened the presidential social scene that he credited her with securing the annexation of Texas. When he gave her the pen with which he signed the Texas bill, she put it on a chain and wore it proudly around her neck.

Painting by G.T.A. Healy

HIGH-LIFE AT PALM BEACH

enry Flagler's Ponce de Leon hotel in St. Augustine opened in late 1888 and was an overnight sensation. In 1894, driving further into the deep South part of Florida, he opened the Royal Poinciana. He had seen the Lake Worth area in 1892 and was intrigued by the palms growing everywhere, sprouted from coconuts that had washed ashore from a shipwreck in 1878. Palm Beach lay 1400 miles further south than the Riviera; people would come to play. And pay. Thus, Palm Beach was to become the playground for the wealthy.

The Palm Beach Inn, later called the Breakers, opened in 1895. But it was for his third wife that Flagler built his masterpiece, Whitehall. All marble, it cost a heady four million, and Mary Lily Flagler's entertaining was more than a match for the setting as it became the scene of many parties.

SPANISH GAZPACHO
LOBSTER-STUFFED TENDERLOIN OF BEEF
PERSIAN RICE
PORTS OF CALL SALAD
COCONUT ICE CREAM * FRENCH LACE COOKIES

Serves 6 to 8

SPANISH GAZPACHO

4 medium tomatoes, peeled and chopped
1 large cucumber, peeled and cubed
1 large onion, chopped
1 large green pepper, chopped
2 (12-ounce) cans tomato juice, divided
⅓ cup olive oil
⅓ cup red wine vinegar
¼ teaspoon hot sauce
1½ teaspoons salt
⅛ teaspoon pepper
2 cloves garlic, peeled and halved
2 tablespoons olive oil
2 slices white bread, cut into ¼-inch cubes
½ cup chopped chives

Combine half of each of the tomato, cucumber, onion, and green pepper in a large bowl. Add ½ cup tomato juice; mix well. Puree vegetable mixture in blender.

Place remaining half of vegetables in separate serving bowls; cover and refrigerate.

Combine pureed vegetables, remaining tomato juice, ⅓ cup olive oil, vinegar, hot sauce, salt, and pepper in a large bowl, mixing well. Cover, and refrigerate at least 3 hours.

Rub inside of small skillet with halved garlic cloves; reserve garlic. Place 2 tablespoons olive oil in skillet, and sauté bread cubes over medium heat until golden brown. Drain well; place in a small serving dish.

To serve, mince reserved garlic; stir into chilled soup mixture, and sprinkle with chives. On a tray, arrange chopped vegetables and croutons to be sprinkled over the top of each serving. Yield: 6 cups.

H.M. Flagler, foremost developer of Southern Florida, and his wife entertained on a lavish scale. Pictured (left) is a party in the Royal Poinciana Hotel's Cocoanut Grove at Palm Beach.

Lobster-Stuffed Tenderloin of Beef on Persian Rice; Spanish Gazpacho.

LOBSTER-STUFFED TENDERLOIN OF BEEF

2 lobster tails
½ teaspoon salt
1 (3-pound) whole beef tenderloin
1 tablespoon butter or margarine, melted
1½ teaspoons lemon juice
6 slices bacon
½ cup chopped green onion
⅛ teaspoon minced garlic
½ cup butter or margarine
½ cup dry white wine
Fresh parsley sprigs (optional)
Whole mushrooms (optional)
Tomato roses (optional)

Place lobster tails and salt in a medium saucepan, and cover with water. Bring to a boil; reduce heat, and simmer 5 minutes. Carefully remove lobster tails from shells. Cut each piece of lobster tail meat in half lengthwise, and set aside.

Cut a horizontal pocket to within ½-inch of opposite side of tenderloin, slicing entire length of tenderloin. Carefully stuff lobster, end to end, inside tenderloin. Combine melted butter and lemon juice; drizzle on lobster. Bind meat with cord or skewers to secure opening. Transfer tenderloin to rack in a broiler pan, and set aside.

Cook bacon in a skillet until crisp; drain, reserving drippings. Crumble bacon; set aside.

Brush entire surface of tenderloin with bacon drippings. Insert meat thermometer in tenderloin, making sure it does not touch roasting pan. Bake at 400° for 25 minutes, or until thermometer registers 130° (rare). Sprinkle top of meat with crumbled bacon.

Sauté green onion and garlic in ½ cup butter. Add wine, and heat thoroughly. Serve sauce with sliced tenderloin. Garnish with parsley sprigs, mushrooms, and tomato roses, if desired. Yield: 8 servings.

PERSIAN RICE

2 tablespoons butter
1⅓ cups uncooked rice
1 teaspoon salt
¾ cup raisins
2 cups chicken broth
1 cup orange juice
1 tablespoon chopped fresh
   parsley
¼ teaspoon grated orange rind
¼ cup slivered almonds,
   toasted

Melt butter in a small Dutch oven over medium heat. Add rice; cook, stirring constantly, until rice is lightly browned. Add next 4 ingredients; bring to a boil. Reduce heat; cover, and simmer 20 minutes. Remove from heat; let stand 5 minutes. Stir in remaining ingredients. Yield: 6 to 8 servings.

Collection of Bonnie Slotnick

PORTS OF CALL SALAD

2 heads romaine lettuce, torn
1 pound yellow squash, cut
   into julienne strips
½ cup chopped fresh parsley
3 egg yolks
½ cup peanut oil
1 cup mayonnaise
¼ cup buttermilk
2 tablespoons grated
   Parmesan cheese
½ teaspoon dry mustard
½ teaspoon salt
¼ teaspoon pepper
2 tablespoons vinegar
1 tablespoon lemon juice
1½ teaspoons Worcestershire
   sauce
¼ teaspoon hot sauce
½ garlic clove, minced
1 ounce anchovy fillets,
   minced

Combine first 3 ingredients in a large salad bowl, tossing well.

Beat egg yolks until thick and lemon colored. Add oil, 1 tablespoon at a time, to egg yolks, beating constantly until mixture begins to thicken. Add mayonnaise and buttermilk, beating until smooth. Add remaining ingredients, and beat until smooth. Toss dressing with salad. Yield: 8 servings.

COCONUT ICE CREAM

6 cups half-and-half
2 cups milk
1½ cups sugar
⅛ teaspoon salt
5 eggs, beaten
5 egg yolks, beaten
2 cups whipping cream
2 (6-ounce) packages frozen
   coconut, partially thawed
1½ teaspoons vanilla extract
2 teaspoons coconut extract

Combine half-and-half, milk, sugar, and salt in a 4-quart saucepan; cook over medium heat 10 minutes or until thickened, stirring constantly.

Combine eggs and egg yolks. Stir one-fourth of half-and-half mixture into egg mixture. Add to remaining half-and-half mixture, stirring constantly. Cook 1 minute; remove from heat, and let mixture cool.

Beat whipping cream until stiff. Fold cream, coconut, vanilla, and coconut extract into half-and-half mixture. Pour into freezer can of a 1-gallon hand-turned or electric freezer. Freeze according to manufacturer's instructions. Let ripen 1 hour before serving. Yield: 1 gallon.

FRENCH LACE COOKIES

1 cup all-purpose flour
1 cup finely chopped pecans
½ cup butter or margarine
½ cup light corn syrup
⅔ cup firmly packed brown
   sugar

Combine flour and pecans in a large mixing bowl; set aside.

Combine remaining ingredients in a medium saucepan; bring mixture to a boil, and remove from heat. Cool; add to flour mixture, mixing well.

Drop dough by teaspoonfuls, 4 inches apart, onto well-greased cookie sheets. Bake at 325° for 8 to 10 minutes or until lightly browned. Cool 2 minutes before removing from cookie sheets. Yield: about 5 dozen.

AN EVENING AT DUNLEITH MANSION

Dunleith Mansion, originally called Routhlands, stands on a terraced rise near the center of Natchez. The double galleried porch is supported by twenty-six Doric columns, and on the roof are six pedimented dormers. Fire destroyed the original house in 1855, and the Charles G. Dahlgrens built the present house in 1856, using some salvaged lumber. It has passed through several ownerships over the years, including the Joseph N. Carpenter family, who retained it for four generations. Dunleith is now owned by the William F. Heins III family of Conroe, Texas.

TOMATO CAVIAR SALAD
ROAST DUCK, SOUTHERN STYLE
WILD RICE
SOUFFLÉED BROCCOLI
DUNLEITH POTATO BREAD
STRAWBERRY RUM PARFAIT

Serves 8

TOMATO CAVIAR SALAD

9 small tomatoes
Salt
2 (3½-ounce) jars black
   caviar, rinsed and drained
Lettuce leaves
Gargogle Sauce

Slice off top of 8 tomatoes; scoop out pulp, leaving shells intact. Reserve pulp. Sprinkle inside of tomato shells with salt; invert, and drain on paper towels.

Peel remaining tomato. Chop peeled tomato and reserved tomato pulp. Add caviar; mix well. Fill tomato shells with caviar mixture. Serve on lettuce leaves with Gargogle Sauce. Yield: 8 servings.

Gargogle Sauce:

1 cup mayonnaise
½ cup chili sauce
2 teaspoons Worcestershire
   sauce
2 tablespoons minced pearl
   onions
¼ teaspoon paprika

Combine all ingredients, stirring well. Chill thoroughly. Stir well before serving. Yield: about 2 cups.

Tomato Caviar Salad (front). Souffléed Broccoli in skillet.

White Tuscan columns and double galleries surround Dunleith.

ROAST DUCK, SOUTHERN STYLE

4 wild ducks, cleaned
2 teaspoons salt
½ teaspoon pepper
2 tablespoons all-purpose
  flour
1 cup water
2 tablespoons butter or
  margarine, melted
½ cup chopped onion
Lemon slices (optional)
Orange Sauce

Place ducks, breast side up, on a rack in a large roasting pan, folding neck skin under.

Combine salt, pepper, and flour; stir well. Sprinkle ducks with flour mixture. Combine water, butter, and onion; pour into roasting pan. Bake, uncovered, at 400° for 1 hour or until drumsticks and thighs move easily. Garnish with lemon slices, if desired. Serve with Orange Sauce. Yield: 8 servings.

Orange Sauce:

⅔ cup firmly packed brown
  sugar
⅔ cup sugar
2 tablespoons all-purpose
  flour
2 tablespoons grated orange
  rind
2 cups orange juice
Dash of salt

Combine all ingredients in a saucepan; cook over medium heat until thickened. Yield: 2 cups.

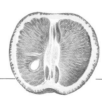

WILD RICE

1 cup uncooked wild rice
½ cup uncooked regular rice
4 (10½-ounce) cans beef
  broth, undiluted
1 cup chopped onion
1 cup chopped green pepper
1 cup fresh mushrooms,
  sliced
¼ cup butter or margarine,
  melted
1 cup whipping cream
1 teaspoon salt
¼ teaspoon pepper

Combine rice and beef broth in a Dutch oven; cook over medium heat until most of the liquid has been absorbed.

Sauté vegetables in butter until tender. Combine with rice and remaining ingredients; stir well. Spoon mixture into a greased 3-quart casserole. Bake at 350° for 20 to 25 minutes. Yield: 8 servings.

SOUFFLÉED BROCCOLI

1 (1½-pound) bunch fresh
  broccoli
½ cup chopped onion
1½ tablespoons vegetable oil
9 eggs, beaten
¼ cup plus 2 tablespoons
  milk
¾ teaspoon garlic salt
¼ teaspoon pepper
¾ cup grated Parmesan
  cheese

Trim off large leaves of broccoli; remove tough ends of lower stalks. Wash broccoli. Remove flowerets. Cook, covered, in a small amount of boiling salted water 5 minutes; drain and set aside.

Sauté onion in oil in a 10-inch skillet until tender. Place broccoli over onion.

Combine eggs, milk, garlic salt, and pepper, mixing well. Pour egg mixture evenly over broccoli. Sprinkle cheese evenly over egg mixture. Cook, covered, over low heat 25 minutes or until set. Cut into wedges, and serve immediately. Yield: 8 to 10 servings.

DUNLEITH POTATO BREAD

1 large potato, peeled and
  diced
1 cup water
1 teaspoon salt
½ cup butter or margarine
½ cup firmly packed brown
  sugar
2 packages dry yeast
¼ cup warm water (105°
  to 115°)
1 teaspoon firmly packed
  brown sugar
½ cup instant nonfat dry
  milk powder
3 eggs, beaten
4½ cups all-purpose flour

Place potato, water, and salt in a small Dutch oven, and bring to a boil. Reduce heat, and cook 15 minutes or until tender. Remove from heat; add butter and ½ cup sugar, stirring well. Allow mixture to cool.

Dissolve yeast in warm water in a large bowl; add 1 teaspoon sugar, and set aside.

Place potato mixture, milk powder, and eggs in container of electric blender; process until mixture is smooth. Combine potato mixture and yeast mixture; stir well. Add flour, stirring well.

Turn dough out onto a floured surface, and knead 8 to 10 minutes or until smooth and elastic. Place in a well-greased bowl, turning to grease top. Cover and let rise in a warm place (85°), free from drafts, 1½ to 2 hours or until doubled in bulk.

Punch dough down; divide into 4 portions. Shape each into a loaf. Place in well-greased 7½- x 3- x 2-inch loafpans. Cover loaves; let rise 45 minutes or until doubled in bulk.

Bake at 375° for 30 minutes or until loaves sound hollow when tapped. Yield: 4 loaves.

STRAWBERRY RUM PARFAIT

6 (10-ounce) packages
  frozen strawberries,
  thawed and
  undrained
1 cup light rum
1 quart vanilla ice
  cream, slightly
  softened
1 cup whipping cream,
  whipped

Soak strawberries in rum overnight.

Spoon about ⅓ cup ice cream into 8 chilled parfait glasses; freeze for 30 minutes. Spoon about 3 tablespoons strawberry mixture over ice cream. Repeat layers. Top with a dollop of whipped cream. Serve immediately. Yield: 8 parfaits.

The steamboat brought an era of prosperity to Mississippi.

Photographer: Noelle Bloom

TEXAS GAME FEAST AT THISTLE HILL

Thistle Hill was originally named Rubusmont, for the purple thistle, a wild flower native to North Central Texas. The English translation became official, although "Rubusmont" is carved over a fireplace in the mansion at 1509 Pennsylvania Avenue in Forth Worth. It was built in 1903 by the W.T. Waggoners for their daughter, Electra, when she married A.B. Wharton. The Whartons sold the house to Winfield Scott in 1911. Scott died, but his widow moved in, and Ft. Worth society reveled in her musicales and wild game menus featuring venison and baked quail.

VENISON ROAST
FRIED QUAIL WITH CREAM GRAVY
SAGE DRESSING
CREAMED ONIONS
CRANBERRY SALAD
SAUERKRAUT RELISH
BAKING POWDER BISCUITS
CHEESE-APPLE PIE

Serves 8

VENISON ROAST

1 medium carrot, scraped and grated
1 cup chopped onion
½ cup chopped parsley
½ cup chopped celery
4 cloves garlic, minced
6 whole cloves
2 slices bacon
2 bay leaves
½ teaspoon salt
½ teaspoon pepper
1 (3- to 4-pound) venison roast
2 cups vegetable oil
3 cups dry white wine

Combine first 10 ingredients. Place half of mixture in a 13- x 9- x 2-inch baking pan. Add roast. Spoon remaining mixture over roast.

Combine oil and wine; pour over roast. Cover, and marinate two days in refrigerator, turning occasionally.

Bake at 300° for 2½ to 3 hours or until tender, basting occasionally with pan drippings. Yield: 8 servings.

FRIED QUAIL WITH CREAM GRAVY

16 quail, cleaned
1 tablespoon salt, divided
1½ teaspoons pepper, divided
2 cups all-purpose flour
Vegetable oil
1½ cups water
¼ cup plus 2 tablespoons all-purpose flour
2 cups milk

Sprinkle quail with 2 teaspoons salt and ½ teaspoon pepper. Dredge in 2 cups flour. Heat oil to 400°, and brown quail on both sides in a large skillet. Pour water over quail. Reduce heat; cover, and cook 10 minutes. Uncover, and simmer an additional 35 minutes. Remove quail to serving platter. Drain off drippings, reserving 6 tablespoons in skillet.

Add remaining flour to reserved drippings; cook over low heat, stirring until smooth. Cook 1 minute, stirring constantly. Gradually add milk; cook over medium heat, stirring constantly, until thickened and bubbly. Stir in remaining salt and pepper. Serve gravy with quail. Yield: 8 servings.

SAGE DRESSING

3½ cups cornbread crumbs
3½ cups soft breadcrumbs
2 cups hot chicken broth
½ cup milk
1 cup chopped celery
3 tablespoons minced onion
¼ cup butter or margarine
2 teaspoons salt
2 to 3 teaspoons rubbed sage
½ teaspoon ground savory seasoning
½ teaspoon pepper
1 egg beaten

Combine cornbread crumbs and breadcrumbs in a large bowl. Pour chicken broth and milk over crumb mixture, stirring well.

Sauté celery and onion in butter until tender; add to crumb mixture, stirring well. Stir remaining ingredients into crumb mixture. Spoon into a lightly greased, shallow 2-quart casserole. Cover; bake at 400° for 15 minutes or until thoroughly heated. Yield: 8 servings.

Texas Game Feast featuring Venison Roast, Fried Quail, and complementary dishes.

CREAMED ONIONS

6 medium onions, sliced
¼ cup butter or margarine
¼ cup all-purpose flour
2 cups milk
1 teaspoon salt
Fresh parsley sprigs

Sauté onion in butter in a large skillet until tender. Remove onion from skillet, and set aside.

Add flour to pan drippings, stirring until smooth. Cook 1 minute, stirring constantly. Gradually add milk; cook over medium heat, stirring constantly, until thickened and bubbly. Stir in salt. Add onion, stirring gently. Garnish with parsley. Yield: 8 servings.

Nineteenth-century engraving of a festive dinner party—even the children take part at their own table.

CRANBERRY SALAD

2 cups fresh cranberries, ground
1 cup sugar
1 (3-ounce) package raspberry-flavored gelatin
1¼ cups boiling water
1 medium apple, diced
1 large orange, peeled, seeded, and ground
8 large marshmallows, quartered
1 cup finely chopped pecans
Lettuce leaves
Mayonnaise (optional)

Combine cranberries and sugar in a bowl; stir well, and set aside.

Dissolve gelatin in boiling water; chill until consistency of unbeaten egg white.

Add cranberry mixture, apple, orange, marshmallows, and pecans to gelatin mixture; mix well. Pour into a lightly oiled 5-cup mold; chill until set. Unmold on lettuce leaves. Garnish with a dollop of mayonnaise, if desired. Yield: 13 servings.

SAUERKRAUT RELISH

1 (16-ounce) can sauerkraut, drained
1 large onion, coarsely chopped
½ cup chopped green pepper
1 (2-ounce) jar chopped pimientos, drained
1 cup sugar
1 cup cider vinegar

Combine all ingredients in a large bowl, and toss until well blended. Cover tightly, and refrigerate at least 24 hours. Yield: 4 cups.

W.T. Waggoner, early cattle baron, built Thistle Hill mansion in 1903.

BAKING POWDER BISCUITS

2 cups all-purpose flour
1 tablespoon baking
  powder
½ teaspoon salt
⅓ cup shortening
¾ to 1 cup milk

Combine flour, baking powder, and salt; stir well. Cut in shortening with pastry blender until mixture resembles coarse meal. Sprinkle milk evenly over flour mixture, stirring until dry ingredients are moistened. Turn dough out onto a lightly floured surface; knead lightly 10 to 12 times.

Pat dough out to ½-inch thickness; cut with a 2½-inch biscuit cutter. Place biscuits on a lightly greased baking sheet. Bake at 450° for 12 minutes or until tops are lightly browned. Yield: 1 dozen.

CHEESE-APPLE PIE

5 cups thinly sliced, unpeeled
  cooking apples
⅔ cup sugar
½ cup all-purpose flour
¾ teaspoon ground cinnamon
Dash of salt
Cheese Pastry
Streusel Topping

Combine apples, sugar, flour, cinnamon, and salt; mix well.
Spoon filling evenly into Cheese Pastry shell, and sprinkle with Streusel Topping. Bake at 425° for 30 minutes or until lightly browned. Yield: one 9-inch pie.

Cheese Pastry:

1 cup all-purpose flour
½ teaspoon salt
¼ cup shortening
¼ cup (1 ounce) shredded
  sharp Cheddar cheese
3 to 4 tablespoons cold water

Combine flour and salt; cut in shortening and cheese with pastry blender until mixture resembles coarse meal. Sprinkle cold water evenly over surface; stir with a fork until all dry ingredients are moistened. Shape dough into a ball; chill. Roll dough out to ⅛-inch thickness on a lightly floured surface. Fit pastry into a 9-inch pieplate. Yield: one 9-inch pastry shell.

Streusel Topping:

½ cup sugar
½ cup all-purpose flour
¼ teaspoon salt
⅓ cup butter or margarine
1 cup (4 ounces) shredded
  sharp Cheddar cheese

Combine first 3 ingredients; cut in butter and cheese with pastry blender until mixture resembles coarse meal. Sprinkle over apples in pastry shell. Yield: enough for one 9-inch pie.

⸞ACKNOWLEDGMENTS

Copy Photographers

David R. Allison
Tom Rose

Recipe Credits

Amandine Chicken Sandwiches, Caraway Cheese Mound, Cucumber-Cheese Sandwiches, Sausage Swirls, Smoked Turkey Rolls adapted from *Atlanta Cooks for Company*, compiled by The Junior Associates of the Atlanta Music Club, Atlanta, Georgia. Published 1968 by Conger Printing Company, Atlanta. By permission of the Atlanta Music Club.

Avocado Mousse, Chicken Salad, Chicken Velvet Soup, Mimosa Champagne Cocktail, Our Famous Popovers, Soufflé of Caramel, Veal Pedernales with Glazed Apples adapted from *Neiman-Marcus—A Taste of the Past*, Neiman-Marcus, Dallas, Texas. By permission of Neiman-Marcus.

Baked Stuffed Red Snapper adapted from *The Jackson Cookbook*, compiled by Symphony League of Jackson, Jackson, Mississippi, © 1971. By permission of Symphony League of Jackson.

Barbecued Pot Roast, Buttered Beets adapted from *Grace Hartley's Southern Cookbook*, collected from the *Atlanta Journal*, Atlanta, Georgia. By permission of Doubleday & Co., Inc., © 1976 by Grace Hartley.

Bass à la Brin, Compote Amulet, Potato Marraine, Melrose Pudding, Riz Isle Brevelle adapted from *Melrose Plantation Cookbook* by Francois Mignon and Clementine Hunter, © 1978. By permission of Mrs. R.B. Williams, Natchitoches, Louisiana.

Berry Roly-Poly, Crab Royal, Creamed Lump Crab, Macaroons, Pork Loin Roast, Raspberry Fool adapted from *Maryland's Way* by Mrs. Lewis R. Andrews and Mrs. J. Reaney Kelly. By permission of The Hammond-Harwood House Association, Annapolis, Maryland, © 1966.

Blancmange, Brandied Peaches, Macaroni Pudding adapted from *Thomas Jefferson's Cookbook* by Marie Kimball. By permission of University Press of Virginia, © 1979.

Broccoli with Hollandaise Sauce, Creamed Chicken, Creamy Potato Casserole, Crystallized Rose Petals & Mint Leaves, Date Squares, Grapefruit-Avocado Salad, Heart and Diamond Sandwiches, Hot Spiced Punch, Meringue Bars, Old-Fashioned Boiled Coffee, Pomegranate Ice, Ribbon Sandwich Loaf, Roast Duck, Southern Style, Sicilian Ice, Tea Punch, Watermelon Ice adapted from the *The Gardeners' Cook Book*, edited by Mildred W. Schlumpf. © 1945 by The Houston Council of Texas Garden Clubs, Inc.

Broiled Oysters, Creole Canapes, Gumbo Filé, Red Beans and Rice adapted from *The Picayune's Creole Cook Book*. Published by The Times-Picayune Publishing Company, © 1936.

Butterhorns adapted from *James K. Polk Cookbook*, compiled by the James K. Polk Memorial Auxiliary, Columbia, Tennessee, © 1978. By permission of the James K. Polk Memorial Auxiliary.

Cabbage Salad, Citron Tarts, Moravian Spiced Apples adapted from *North Carolina and Old Salem Cookery* by Elizabeth Hedgecock Sparks, © 1955. By permission of Elizabeth Hedgecock Sparks.

Carrot Ring Mold, Cold Cucumber Soup, Crisp Corn Sticks, Green Peas, Plantation Shrimp Pilau, Lemon Cream Meringue adapted from *Charleston Receipts* by The Junior League of Charleston, South Carolina, © 1950. By permission of The Junior League of Charleston.

Charleston Oyster Soup adapted from *Two Hundred Years of Charleston Cooking*, edited by Lettie Gay, © 1976. By permission of the University of South Carolina Press.

Cherry Ice, Melting Dreams, Minted Green Peas, October Cider Cake, Stuffed Dates, Tropical Mint Punch adapted from *Aunt Hank's Rock House Kitchen*, compiled by Georgia Mae Smith Ericson. By permission of Crosby County Pioneer Memorial Museum, Crosbyton, Texas, © 1977.

Chicken and Country Ham Deep Dish Pie, Ducklings with Apples and Raisins, Persimmon Pudding adapted from *Thirteen Colonies Cookbook* by Donovan, Hatrack, Mills, and Shull. By permission of Praeger, Inc., © 1975.

Coconut Ice Cream, French Lace Cookies, Lobster-Stuffed Tenderloin of Beef, Persian Rice, Ports of Call Salad, Spanish Gazpacho adapted from *Palm Beach Entertains* by The Junior League of the Palm Beaches, Inc., Palm Beach, Florida, © 1976. By permission of The Junior League of the Palm Beaches, Inc.

Corn Pone, Sassafras Tea, Squaw Bread, Wilted Watercress Salad adapted from *Cherokee Cookbook,* compiled by Jack Baker. © 1968 by the Indian Heritage Association. By permission of Cherokee Nation, Tahlequah, Oklahoma.

Country Steak, German Potato Salad, Relish Bowl, Shaker Wheaten Bread, Spiced Tomato Juice, Strawberry Preserves adapted from *We Make You Kindly Welcome* by Elizabeth C. Kremer. Published by Shakertown Pleasant Hill Press, © 1970. By permission of Shakertown at Pleasant Hill, Harrodsburg, Kentucky.

Cucumber Aspic adapted from *Southern Sideboards* by the Junior League of Jackson, Mississippi, © 1978. By permission of the Junior League of Jackson.

Dunleith Potato Bread, Strawberry Rum Parfait adapted from *Dunleith Mansion Collection,* compiled by The Pilgrimage Garden Club, Natchez, Mississippi. By permission of The Natchez Pilgrimage Garden Club.

Fried Apple Pies courtesy of Mrs. V.A. Murdoch, Dallas, Texas.

Monticello Gumbo, Vanilla Ice Cream adapted from *The Monticello Cookbook* by The University of Virginia Hospital Circle.

Homemade Egg Noodles, Poppy Seed Cake adapted from *Guten Appetit!,* compiled by the Sophienburg Memorial Association, Inc., New Braunfels, Texas, © 1978. By permission of Sophienburg Museum.

Lafayette Gingerbread adapted from *LaFayette Ginger Bread,* by Mary Ball Washington. © 1924 by the Washington-Lewis Chapter, D.A.R., Fredericksburg, Virginia.

Old-Time Apple Pie adapted from *The Nashville Cookbook,* compiled by Nashville Area Home Economics Association, Nashville, Tennessee. By permission of Nashville Area Home Economics Association.

Pecan Pie courtesy of Mrs. Clint Wyrick, Garland, Texas.

Rack of Lamb de Simone courtesy of The Park Avenue Room, Skirvin Plaza Hotel, Oklahoma City, Oklahoma.

Ramos Gin Fizz, Sazerac Cocktail adapted from *Brennan's New Orleans Cookbook.* © 1961 by Brennan's Restaurant and Hermann B. Deutsch. By permission of Mr. David C. Wilson.

S&S Cinnamon Rolls courtesy of the S&S Tea Room, Dallas, Texas, Mrs. Barbara Fisher, Owner.

Steamed Chicken and Gravy adapted from *Purefoy Hotel Cook Book* by Eva B. Purefoy, Talladega, Alabama.

Sourdough Biscuits courtesy or Mrs. Vernice Maples, Dallas, Texas.

Venison Roast adapted from *The Texas Wild Game Cookbook* by Judith and Richard Morehead. Printed 1972 by The Encino Press, Austin, Texas. By permission of Judith and Richard Morehead.

Text Credits

Page references in parentheses indicate where material appears in this volume.

Andrews, Mrs. Lewis R., and Mrs. J. Reaney Kelly. *Maryland's Way.* Annapolis: The Hammond-Harwood House Association, 1963. (93,106)

Baer, Evelyn D. "Cownes: A Reminiscence." *Virginia Cavalcade,* Summer, 1982. (43)

"Bridge Party at Ashton Villa" courtesy of Ashton Villa, Galveston, Texas. (80)

Colonial Williamsburg Research Foundation, Research Center, Williamsburg, Virginia. (106)

Kremer, Elizabeth. *Welcome Back to Pleasant Hill.* Harrodsburg: Sharkertown Pleasant Hill Press, 1977. (43)

Morgan, Sarah. *Dining with the Cattle Barons.* Waco: Texian Press, 1981. (7,112)

Sibley, Celestine. "Southern Journal." *Southern Living,* May, 1982. (43,100)

Spitzmiller, Mary Martha Lybrook. *Heritage of Hospitality.* Winston-Salem: Junior League of Winston-Salem, 1975. (52,74)

Collection of Bonnie Slotnick

INDEX

THE Magazine For You
if You Share Our Interest
in the South.

SOUTHERN LIVING
features articles to help make
life for you and your
family more comfortable,
more stimulating, more fun...

SOUTHERN LIVING is about your home and how to make a
more attractive, more convenient, more comfortable place to
live. Each issue brings you dozens of decorating and remodeling
ideas you can adapt to your own surroundings.

SOUTHERN LIVING is about gardening and landscaping and
how to make the outside of your home just as attractive as the
inside. In addition to gardening features, you'll find a monthly
garden calendar pinpointing what to plant and when, plus a
"Letters to our Garden Editor" section to answer your own
particular questions.

SOUTHERN LIVING is about good food and entertaining, with
recipes and menu ideas that are sure to delight your family and
friends. You'll discover recipes with a Southern accent from
some of the South's superlative cooks.

SOUTHERN LIVING is about travel and just plain fun. Every
new issue offers an information-packed monthly calendar of
special events and happenings throughout the South, plus
features on the many fascinating places of interest the South has
to offer.

To find out how you can receive SOUTHERN LIVING every
month, simply write to: SOUTHERN LIVING, P. O. Box
C-119, Birmingham, AL 35283.